ROOTS

IN

INDIANA

HEATHER WATKINS

BLACK ROSE
writing™

© 2014 by Heather Watkins

All rights reserved. No part of this book may be reproduced, stored in a retrieval system or transmitted in any form or by any means without the prior written permission of the publishers, except by a reviewer who may quote brief passages in a review to be printed in a newspaper, magazine or journal.

The final approval for this literary material is granted by the author.

First printing

Most characters appearing in this work are fictitious unless referred to by factual name. Any resemblance to real persons, living or dead, unless explicitly stated, is purely coincidental.

ISBN: 978-1-61296-367-9

PUBLISHED BY BLACK ROSE WRITING

www.blackrosewriting.com

Printed in the United States of America

Roots in Indiana is printed in Adobe Caslon Pro

ACKNOWLEDGMENT

In order to live out your dream, finding inspiration is key. It was my late grandmother, Wilma Jean Garufi, who inspired me to write this book. No matter how ambitious my dreams were as a young girl, she was my biggest fan. My grandmother had faith in me, especially when I felt lost. It was her strength that taught me how to carry on and never give up until I found my way. She had a few rough patches in her own life and battled medical issues as she got older, but those who knew her would describe her as always smiling and full of cheer. Her selflessness was admirable, as she supported many different charities and was active within her community. Family was important to her and she made all of us feel incredibly loved. If you ask my family what they miss most about her, their answer would be simple: her hugs. Without her, I wouldn't be the woman I am today. She was a "people person" and made friends everywhere she went. I'd like to think I'm following in her footsteps.

Roots in Indiana is a story that came to me as I mourned the loss of the most remarkable woman I'd ever known. Although my grandmother isn't here to celebrate the success of my first novel, I know she was right there beside me as the words poured out from my heart. I hope this book will teach my children that they should follow their own dreams and never stop until they cross that finish line.

Piercing through the heart of this story is the message that even though families sometimes disagree or suffer through difficult times, somehow love will always lead them right back home where they belong.

A special thanks to Lisa Petrocelli and to all my family and friends, I value the love and support you continuously give to me. I am a blessed woman.

ROOTS

IN

INDIANA

CHAPTER ONE

When my mother wasn't performing her maternal role, which was quite often, it was my grandmother who played the part.

"It doesn't look good," my father said with a tremble in his voice.

As I put down my cell phone, I could feel my stomach twist and turn, like someone was churning butter with my insides. I rushed to get into the car, thinking about my Nanny lying unconscious in the hospital, and I wondered if this was it. *Nah, it can't be. She's always been a strong woman and has looked after me my whole life. This can't be the end for her. Not yet!*

As I raced through a yellow light, fearful emotions were taking over and I barely caught enough air to breathe. I had to get there so I could hold her hand.

I found a parking spot directly in the front of the Emergency Room door and rushed inside. I asked the young Hispanic woman sitting at the information desk where I could locate my grandmother. I had such trepidation that I completely forgot to mention what her actual name was. My mind was scattered, my heart pounding, and a lump was growing in my throat.

"Corolla. Her last name is Corolla," I finally blurted out as the woman stared at me blankly.

"Ah yes, please follow me. You can join the rest of her visitors in the family room," she said with an accent.

Family room? This can't be a good sign.

"Is everything okay with her?" I asked nervously.

"I am not sure about the details of our patients. Mrs. Corolla has a lot of visitors so we had to put you in a separate room," she explained as she opened the door for me.

The first person I saw, sitting on a rose-colored love seat, her eyes filled with tears, was my Aunt Sharon. This is serious. The atmosphere was somber and I could almost feel the collective worry in the air. I had a feeling that this may end up being the worst day of my life. I walked to my aunt and hugged her tightly as I sat down next to her.

"It's not good," she cried out as an eruption of tears rushed down her cheek. I tried to remain calm because I was still trying to figure out what happened.

"Who said it's not good?" I asked.

She wiped away her tears so she could talk with me. "The doctor told us she was bleeding on her brain. When I took her to chemo a few months back, Dr. Kapoor told me that if a patient suffering from Myelodysplastic Syndrome develops bleeding on the brain, there is nothing else they can do for them."

"I'm not sure I understand. How did she start bleeding on her brain?"

"Poppy said she got out of bed this morning and started walking down the hallway and just collapsed. When she fell, she must have hit her head, which caused the bleeding."

I put my head in my hands. I had called my grandmother that morning. In fact, I called her every day to say good morning. She usually responded, "What's so good about it?" I would then explain to her that it's a great morning because I could talk to her and tell her how much I loved her. But this particular morning when I called, there was no answer. I had just assumed she was in the bathroom or maybe putting the pot of coffee on for my grandfather. It never occurred to me that something may have happened to her.

I picked my head up and looked around the room. My cousin Ben, Aunt Sharon's son, was sitting in a chair completely mute, staring at his phone. My Aunt Vivian was sitting across the room next to my grandfather. She was rubbing his back, telling him that everything would be okay. From the look on his face, I don't think he believed her.

Watching my grandfather sit there put a wound in my heart. My grandparents have been married for fifty-seven years and have always taught us to have strong family values. My grandmother, who has been the bonding agent of our family, always took care of her husband. What would he do without her?

No, she's going to make it, I thought to myself. *I don't care what Dr. Kapoor says.* Doctors make mistakes all the time. Only God can decide if a person is going to live or die. He wouldn't take her yet. She hasn't seen me graduate from college or get married. My grandmother needed more time.

A part of me was trying to justify my feelings with God. I started to pray and explain all the reasons why we needed her here. She wanted to go back to Indiana where she grew up. Her illness was preventing her from taking the trip but as soon as she felt better I was going to take her.

My dad was walking toward me. I hadn't talked to him yet because he was on the phone with my mother when I arrived.

"Hi Daddy," I said, hugging him as tight as my arms would allow.

"Anna, you really should be in class right now," he replied.

"Dad, I need to be here. If I was in class I wouldn't be paying attention," I explained.

"I understand, sweetheart, but you only have another month till graduation," he said as he took a tissue from out of his pocket and wiped his nose.

"Exactly Dad, I am almost finished and this will not affect graduation at all. There is no place I'd rather be right now than with my family. Speaking of family, where is Mom?" I asked.

"She is caught up in meetings, Anna, but will try to come by later."

Ugh! I was so tired of my mother making up excuses. She needed to be here for my father and for me. But it's "Thirsty Thursday," so I was certain a Happy Hour was on her agenda. I walked over to where my Aunt Sharon was and sat down. My mother wasn't going to get any of my attention. What kind of wife doesn't put her family first? My grandmother always had. That's why she was more of a mother to me than the woman who gave birth to me.

I started thinking about my grandmother more and more. I had visited her two days prior. She wasn't feeling well. Her left eye showed signs of blood, but she assumed it was a broken blood vessel. What really worried me was when she explained how she could taste metal in her mouth. I should have known all these signs were not good. I called her doctor's office that day and they told me to make sure she got to the hospital for a checkup. Aunt Sharon left work early to take her. When I left my grandmother's house that day she gave me a hug and said, "Well, if I don't make it, you know I love you." I simply replied, "I love you too, and if that's the case you better haunt me." I was half joking. Never in a million years would I have thought I'd be sitting in an Emergency Room only two days later. I knew she wasn't well, but she always found a way to bounce back up from tumbling down.

Maybe she knew she was going to die. Why didn't I say all the things I should have said? I regretted not telling her how much better my life was because she was in it. My grandmother was the woman who always made any sorrow turn into a warm spring day just by wrapping her arms around you. While my mother was busy drinking with her entourage of single girlfriends, wishing she was twenty-five again, my grandmother was busy combing and braiding my hair for school. I was blessed to have her in my life and I wasn't prepared to let go.

Suddenly we heard a knock at the door. A middle-aged man with grey highlights walked in wearing a long white doctor's coat. The name "Dr. Carle" in blue letters was embroidered on the pocket of his left breast.

"Good Afternoon, my name is Dr. Carle, and I am the neurosurgeon here at St. Francis."

My Aunt Vivian spoke right up. "Do we know what is happening to my mother?"

"Yes. Your mother has internal bleeding on the right side of her brain. I am making an assumption that she possibly has suffered a small stroke, but I won't be able to confirm that until we run some more tests. What we do need to decide is if you'd like us to operate or not."

"Operate or not?" asked my Aunt Sharon. "What happens if we don't operate?"

Dr. Carle simply said, "She will die." He could tell that we were all stunned, so he further explained the situation.

"In this circumstance, if we operate, she has a fifty-fifty chance of survival. If she makes it through surgery and wakes up, there will be some sort of impediment with her brain functionality."

"So what you are saying is that my mother will either survive this surgery and have a disability—or die?" Aunt Sharon asked, but she could barely make out the words before more tears fell from her dark brown eyes.

"I'm sorry I don't have better news for you. I understand this is something you will need to discuss as a family before we proceed," Dr. Carle explained.

"Would you do the surgery if she was *your* mother?" Aunt Vivian asked the doctor.

He took a deep breath and said, "No, I wouldn't. Personally, I couldn't see putting my mother through that but this ultimately is your choice."

I didn't like Doctor Carle. He lacked in bedside manners. I understand doctors have to be careful with the information they convey but his reply seemed so shallow. The man said it himself that she had a fifty-fifty chance of survival. They weren't exactly the words I was hoping to hear, but I'd take my chances on those odds.

It was now up to my grandfather to decide whether or not he would want to put his wife through this risky operation. As I glanced over at him, I wanted to cry some more. How do you make a decision like that? Both my aunts went over to him to talk it through. My dad stood behind them without saying much.

"I'll give you all a few minutes to decide how we should move forward. If you choose to go forward with the surgery, I will need to prepare a team. I'll just be waiting right outside," said Dr. Carle as he walked out of the room.

I started to worry. What if she made it through surgery and then didn't recognize us? Would she be a completely different person? Would she still be able to walk or talk? On the flip side, if we just let her be, she will eventually die. None of these options were playing out in our favor. It was the worst day of my life. I walked out into the hallway with my cousin Ben so our parents could discuss the options in private. The doctor was also waiting in the hallway with us.

"Fifty-fifty are pretty good odds," I said to him.

"Depends on how you look at it," he replied in a cold tone.

"I understand she can be different afterward, but don't you at least have to try and save the one you love? Ultimately, it's in God's hands," I explained.

"This is why it is important for your family to discuss the options. We give our medical opinion but the choice isn't ours. As for God, if your family has a strong belief, I suggest you start praying."

What? Did this doctor really just say that? I was standing in a religious hospital, hence the name St. Francis.

"If you don't have faith in the surgery, then why give it such decent odds?" Ben questioned.

"Because the chances of her recovering the way she once was are slim. Her brain has suffered and she probably will not be the same person you knew her to be. She could survive; however, based on the tests, her quality of life may not be good," he tried to explain.

Ben looked disgusted with his unsympathetic answers.

I then looked at the doctor and said, "Well, with all due respect, sir, my grandmother is an extraordinary woman and I know she would give it a good fight."

"I can only state the facts, young lady," he said as he looked through the papers on his clipboard.

The door opened to the family room and my Aunt Vivian signaled the doctor back in. Ben and I followed.

"Have we made a decision?" asked Dr. Carle.

"We have," my Aunt Vivian replied. "We are going ahead with the surgery."

"Alright, I will go and prepare a team for the operation. As soon as the details are set, I will send a nurse with further instructions. For now, you are welcome to stay here."

"Thank you doctor," my grandpa said with sadness in his voice.

"Can I go see my grandmother?" I asked Dr. Carle. *I had to see her!*

"Sure, if you walk down the hallway, she is in the very last room. You will see the word 'Triage' on the door," he said as he pointed toward the hall.

I started walking down the hallway. As I got closer to the room, I felt the walls closing in on me. I kept praying that any minute now I would wake up and realize none of this was real. I so badly wished that I was at her house doing crossword puzzles with her. She'd be up all hours of the night playing those to avoid the pain in her legs from the neuropathy. She rarely slept in a bed because it was too painful. Thinking about all of this was making me angry with God. My grandmother was always a saint and this was her reward? It seemed so unfair.

I walked into the triage room and tears filled my eyes. My vision was blurry as I moved closer to the table she was lying on. My grandmother's neck was secured in a brace and her eyes were closed. She had tubes down her throat, helping her breathe. Not only were the tears falling from my eyes, but from my heart too. I wanted to set her free from this confinement. I kept praying that she would open her eyes and say, "Anna Banana, it's going to be okay." Instead, I watched her chest move as she struggled with each breath. I took her hand and covered it with mine.

"Hi Nanny, it's Anna. I wanted to see you," I tried so hard to speak. My voice was crackling as the tears released from my emerald eyes. "I hope you can hear me. You have to go through an operation and it won't be easy. I know everything in your life has been a hard journey. You're always the one who said God only gives us what we can handle. I don't think I can handle losing you. Not yet. Remember you told me you still had things you wanted to do here. I hope that God grants you more time with us. I know you have family in Heaven you would want to see but I'm really hoping they can wait awhile longer. I can't imagine you not being here for things like my college graduation or even my wedding." My tears kept dripping like a leaky faucet.

"I don't know where I would have been if it weren't for you taking care of me all these years. You deserve more time and I pray you get it, Nanny."

I stood over her and gently kissed her forehead. If only I could feel one of her hugs, I know it would make this all better. I was having a hard time letting go of her hand. I wondered if it would be the last time I would feel her warm hand in mine.

"I love you Nanny, and you're still the prettiest little old lady around," I said as I gazed down at her one more time.

Dr. Carle came back to the family room just as I was walking in.

"The operation should take about four hours. You are welcome to go up to the fifth floor waiting area and I will send a nurse out during the procedure to give updates to your family. Do you have any further questions before we get started?" the doctor asked.

My Aunt Vivian raised her hand to question the doctor. "When will we know if the surgery was successful?"

"We can't be sure. If she wakes up, we will run tests to see how much brain function has been lost. If she does not wake up within twenty-four hours, then we will proceed with a CAT scan on the brain to see where we stand. Does that answer your question?"

"Yes, thank you doctor," Aunt Vivian replied.

* * *

I stared up at the clock. It was 3:00 p.m. and she'd only been in the operating room for forty-five minutes. I thought about her laying there in the hands of Dr. Carle, the bitter man who said he wouldn't put his own mother through the operation. Was he right? Maybe she was already gone and we were prolonging the inevitable. I tried to shake off my dreadful thoughts. I wanted to have faith, but it was such an intangible thing.

My grandmother went to church faithfully every Sunday. She'd put fifty dollars a week into that church basket as a donation. In fact, she donated to every charity that came through the mail. That was her, always trying to save the world, feed the hungry, and cure all illnesses. Yet, here she was fighting for her own life. The only ones who could help her were a team of doctors and God. I felt helpless knowing that I couldn't do anything to save her. That was the thing with life and death —they are uncontrollable. You can't escape death. Why would God save my grandmother when there were children with cancer fighting for their lives? How did he choose which people got to live and which ones went up to Heaven with him? My mind was a whirlwind and I had to take a walk.

"I'm going to get a coffee. Does anyone else want one?" I asked.

"I'll go," Ben said as he got up from the couch.

Ben worked for an elite brokerage firm and already owned his own home. I was two years older than him but it seemed as if he had lived longer. He studied abroad at Oxford for a semester and went backpacking across Europe last fall. I never traveled much. The last family vacation we had was when I was nine. It was a cruise to the Caribbean but soon after that my mom fell in love with something called "Johnny Walker." I kept telling myself that once college was over I would have an "adventure."

"I could really use a coffee. This is torturous," Ben said as we walked on to get our caffeine fix.

"I hate the waiting. It really is the hardest part. I'm nervous to see what happens afterward, like if she will recognize us." I grabbed a Styrofoam cup and handed one to Ben.

"I know what you mean. I can't imagine what it would be like without her here," Ben said in a somber tone.

"Well, let's hope we won't have to," I replied as I poured more sugar into my coffee.

"The doctor didn't seem too confident," Ben said as he almost burnt his lip. "Wow, this coffee is hot."

"They have to be careful what they say these days. He probably doesn't want to give us false hope."

"That's true," said Ben as we walked back over to our family.

There were still no updates on her surgery. I brought a coffee back for my grandfather. I knew he could use one but he didn't drink much of it. His worry was revealed through his dark brown Italian eyes. I couldn't fathom what was going through his mind. Here I was, scared about losing my grandmother, and this man is awaiting the fate of his wife of fifty-seven years. If she doesn't make it, how will he survive without her? She had done everything for him. In fact, I don't think he has ever even made himself a sandwich. That was Nanny though, always taking care of everyone else.

Hour after hour, I sat in that waiting room with my family, and a few other strangers who may have been in a similar situation. I somehow felt tied to those people and wondered if they were also waiting to find out if a loved one would survive.

I looked over at a middle-aged woman. Her hair was a bit messy, tied up in a bun. The wrinkles on her face portrayed the amount of stress in her life. Was she waiting to hear news about her mother, her father, or maybe her husband? Her hands were fidgeting rapidly, almost like she was washing them, only she had no soap. Her right foot was tapping on the floor. Something was definitely antagonizing her. At that moment, I knew we were really not alone. People went through this every day. Everyone has experienced heartache and loss at one time or another, yet somehow the world still had so much hate and violence. We are walking together in the same direction.

As I was engaging in this philosophical conversation in my mind, a nurse, wearing a kind smile and chunky hips, waddled her way over to us.

"Mr. Corolla?" she asked in a soft tone.

"Yes?" my grandfather looked up at her.

"I'm just giving you an update on your wife, Jeanie. She is still in surgery but is stable. The doctors are working really hard to do what they can," she explained.

"So she's still in there?" he asked.

Poor guy, he was old and didn't always comprehend everything. The nurse got a little closer to him and said, "Yes sir, she is, but the doctors say everything is going well."

"How much longer is this going to take?"

When I heard my grandfather say that to the nurse, it broke my heart. I knew he wished he could be in there with her, holding her hand, trying to save her. At least that was how I felt.

"It should be maybe another hour or two at most. Once they are done, they will move her up to the eleventh floor for recovery. We will inform you when that happens," the nurse continued to explain.

My Aunt Vivian signaled the nurse and asked, "Did the doctor say how bad the bleeding is on her brain?"

She was always the spokesperson for the family. I think it was because she was good at setting her emotions aside and focusing on the issue. I wondered how long she could last like that. People needed to cry. Tears produced hormones like prolactin, adrenocorticotropic, and leu-enkephalin, mainly when they were emotionally driven. It helped that I was getting a Masters in Psychology and studied this. I had taken a class called Death and Dying, therefore, I should've been prepared for something like this, but I wasn't.

"I'm not sure about the bleeding, ma'am. The doctor will speak with your family once the operation is complete and can inform you of the details." The nurse sounded aggravated.

In these circumstances it would have been nice to have a compassionate staff. I got it, they deal with it every day and it's hard to show sympathy when you're exposed to these things on a daily basis. I'm sure working in the medical field wasn't easy. I felt my pocket vibrate so I pulled out my phone. I had received a text from my best friend, Chelsea. It read, *"Anna, I heard about Nanny and wanted to see if you needed me to come by the hospital? I get out of work in 20 mins."*

I typed back, *"She is still in surgery, no news yet. I'm scared but hoping for the best. Thanks for offering to come by. I may need you later depending on how this turns out."*

A few moments later, my lap was vibrating again. *"Just call me and I will come right up. Your fam is my fam!"*

That is why Chelsea is my best friend. She always knows exactly what to say. I texted her back, *"Love ya Chels...you are the best!"*

CHAPTER TWO

Waiting was all we could do now. The eleventh floor was dim and quiet. It was where all the critical patients went to recover. My grandmother was out of surgery but hadn't woken up yet. We had the waiting room all to ourselves. It was pitch black outside and every now and then we would hear the Lifestar helicopter take off or land.

Various people had come by to visit—mostly our extended family and close friends. The company distracted us from the constant worry. It was nice to see family we hadn't seen in a long time. That was always how it worked, though. You'd only see distant relatives on certain occasions. My mom stopped by for a little while and then left. The alcohol was probably calling her. I felt bad for my father because she should have been right by his side. For the last few months, I kept telling him that he needed to give her an ultimatum. It had to be either rehab or a divorce. My dad always told me to stay out of things. He didn't want me getting caught up with their marital problems but it was difficult, seeing I lived under the same roof.

As I thought about my mother's lack of support, I started to think about how much impact my grandmother had on my life. She was the best role model and always listened to every idea or dream I had. It was because of her that I would be getting my Masters soon. When I got my Bachelors, she asked me what I wanted to do next. I told her I thought about staying in school and going right for my Masters. She said, "Go do it!" Her tone was far from ordinary. It was full of excitement, as if she herself were taking the same steps with me.

I started thinking about all the things we've done together and how fast time seemed to slip away. The sadness began to swallow me whole.

I already missed seeing her smile and hearing her voice. What if I never heard it again? What if I never felt one of her hugs again? The tears started to fill up inside my eyes. Eventually they ran out of room and began to fall out. My dad walked over to me and put his arm around my shoulder.

"Anna, it's going to be alright," he whispered.

Was it? I wondered.

* * *

Midnight was approaching and I wanted to see her again. I had to push the button by the security door so they would let me in. The floor was beyond protected. It reminded me of the Labor and Delivery section of the hospital. I pressed the buzzer and said, "This is Anna Corolla. I'd like to visit with my grandmother, Jeanie Corolla, please."

I walked by the nurse's station as they were huddled around, conversing amongst each other. They were full of laughter and smiles. I wished I was having that kind of night. Her room was dim and just the light from the hallway shined in. I sat down beside my grandmother and took a deep breath. Her head was wrapped with bandages from the surgery and tubes were still coming out of her mouth, assisting her breathing. I wanted to fix her. It was difficult to see her like this.

It had been a couple of hours and she still showed no signs of movement. The doctor said it would have been better if she had woken up already but maybe she needed more time to rest. I decided to talk to her, hoping she would hear my voice and give me some sort of signal that she was okay.

"You've done good Nanny," I whispered to her. "I'm so proud of you, having to go through all of this. You're a champ." I glanced around the room. There was a painting hanging on the wall of a little girl carrying a basket of flowers. The sun was beaming on her fair skin and she looked at peace.

"I wish I could go back to when I was a little girl. Then you wouldn't be in this bed going through this agony." I started reminiscing with her, hoping my words would wake her somehow.

"Remember when they would play 'How Great Thou Art' in

church and we'd sing together? I know you always loved that song. Then, after church we'd go have breakfast at Denny's. I loved how Poppy would order us french fries and we'd pick out the crunchiest ones to eat first."

I was laughing and crying at the same time while sharing those memories. It was hard to think that maybe there wouldn't be any more to create. I wished I was seven again. When I was a kid, I didn't worry about much. Never did I think about illness or death. The only stressful thing was playing in an all-star softball game or studying for an upcoming math test. I would much rather go through that than this. Being an adult was not fun. I thought I was ready to be one but now I wasn't so sure.

I laid my head down next to my grandmother and felt her chest moving up and down. Teardrops ran down my face and onto her blanket. I was afraid to leave her but my dad poked his head into the room.

"We should go home Anna," he said.

I lifted my head off of my grandmother and got up from my chair. I leaned over and whispered in her ear. "I love you, Nanny. Please don't give up." I then kissed her forehead and walked over to my dad. He put his arms out to hug me. I knew he needed a hug too.

When we got into my dad's car, it was silent. I'm sure he was a bundle of nerves. I kept worrying about what would happen if my grandmother woke up while we were all gone. I didn't want her to be alone.

"It's important for us to get our rest, Anna, and the doctors said they would call the moment she wakes up," my dad said as if he was reading my mind.

"I know, Dad, I just hate leaving her there all alone."

"It'll be okay. It's been a long day and we all need some downtime," he replied, so calm and collected.

My pillow was anything but comfortable that night. I gazed up at my bedroom ceiling. It was filled with fake glow-in-the-dark stars that I bought back in high school. I noticed one was starting to fall off. It reminded me of how life goes by. Nothing lasts forever, not even glow-in- the-dark stars. I turned on my side, hugged the oversized teddy bear my father had bought me for my fifth birthday, and closed my eyes.

* * *

I hadn't pulled down my shades, so the morning sun beamed into my room. I looked at my alarm and noticed it was already 9:30. I wondered if the hospital called. I threw on my robe and ran down the stairs. My father was sitting at the table reading the morning paper while drinking his coffee.

"Any word from the hospital, Dad?" I asked.

He looked disappointed and said, "No, Anna. She is still asleep."

"Shouldn't she have woken up by now?"

"It would have been better if she had. The doctor said they would be running a few tests this morning."

"What kinds of tests?" I asked.

"They will perform a CAT scan to see if there are any signs of activity in her brain."

"What happens if there is no activity?"

"I'm not sure, Anna. Why don't you grab a bagel and we can go back to the hospital," he suggested.

"Okay Dad," I said as I went over to the counter and chose a poppy seed bagel from the bakery bag.

When we arrived back on the eleventh floor, both my aunts were already there. Auntie Sharon was staring out the window, not saying a word. I walked over to her and rubbed her back to let her know I was there.

"The doctor is going to speak with us in twenty minutes. They completed some tests. I'm scared, Anna. What if the results are bad?" she asked with tears in her eyes.

Aunt Sharon looked as if she had been hit by a truck. I don't think she slept a wink last night. I hugged her as tight as my arms would allow. I tried to reassure her that things would be okay. My grandmother always used to say that God only gave us things we could handle. I don't think my coaxing efforts helped but I tried anyway. The more we talked, the more I became worried about the results too.

Aunt Vivian was talking to my dad. I could hear her ask why my mother wasn't with us. She shouldn't be too surprised. My mom barely showed up for family functions, so why would we expect her to appear at the hospital where her mother-in-law might be dying? The more I thought about my mother, the more I started to get angry with her again. My dad deserved better. Everyone had their spouse's support— everyone, except my dad. I loved my mother but was very disappointed.

Just then a nurse came in and walked over to my family.

"Dr. Henry would like to speak with you now in the conference room regarding Mrs. Corolla's results. It's right around the corner. I can take you there," she said as she held the door open for them.

Dr. Henry partnered with Dr. Carle. I had hoped that this doctor would be friendlier than his cohort. I took a seat and felt my heart race as I watched them walk out of the room. *What kind of news did he have? Is it bad? Is she in some sort of coma?*

I had to see her. I knew she would be back in her room since the tests were all done. I once again pushed the button to reach the nurse's station and they buzzed me in. When I walked in to see her, it looked as if she hadn't moved at all. I sat down in the chair beside her bed.

As I watched her sleep, I tried to remain calm. I was scared to find out about the results. She should have been awake by now. It wasn't fair. Why would God do this to such a beautiful soul?

A teardrop danced slowly out of my left eye. I felt it run down my nose and onto my lips. I could taste my own sorrow. I didn't think I had any tears left to cry. I would give anything to see her wake up and smile at me. If only I could hear her voice or feel her arms wrap around me, everything would be better. Her hugs always made me feel like I was a gift. Perhaps it was because I was her only granddaughter.

I thought about a time when I surprised her at the hairdresser and she went on and on about how wonderful I was to her old lady friends. They all had their hair in curlers, sitting under the hair dryer. I was so embarrassed, yet it felt good to know she was proud of me. I don't think I ever heard my own mother brag about me to her friends the way my grandmother did.

"Excuse me miss," a young nurse said, interrupting me from my thoughts. I looked up at her cheerful grin. "I just need to get her vitals," she said.

I kissed my grandmother's cheek and tried to prepare myself for the news ahead of me. I must have whispered a million prayers as I left her room and headed back to the waiting area. *Please be a miracle, please, please, please be a miracle.*

As I turned the corner and glanced into the waiting room, my Aunt Sharon was hugging my grandfather. My Aunt Vivian was on her cell phone with tears streaming down her face. I had a feeling it was bad. I stopped for a moment. I didn't want to move. The longer I stood there, the longer it prevented me from hearing the horrible outcome. I wasn't ready to face it. My father walked over to me. He cleared his throat and said, "I'm so sorry, Anna." He tried hard to block his own sadness.

"The CAT scan showed no brain activity at all," he said.

"So she's going to die?" I asked as the tears began to splurge.

I couldn't believe it. My grandmother was the strongest-willed person I knew. She'd been through a tough childhood and all kinds of health issues. This couldn't beat her. It had to be a mistake.

My dad tried to speak through his weary voice. He explained that she fought as long as she could but the battle had to end sometime. My father was giving up. He had accepted that she was going to die. A part of me knew I had to be realistic too. No matter how badly I wanted my grandmother to prove these doctors and these tests wrong, I had to grow up. I was always more of a dreamer but sometimes that just made life harder.

"How much longer does she have?" I asked.

"Grandpa has to decide if he wants to take her off the respirator," he said.

"You mean 'pull the plug'," I said as I wiped the tears from my eyes.

"Yes Anna. I don't think we are going to make any decisions right now. If she hangs on throughout the night, I think Poppy will stop the respirator in the morning. It's just not fair to keep her stringing along."

"So that's it? What if the CAT scan is wrong? What if we stop the respirator and in reality she had a chance to live? I don't want to stop believing in her, Dad." I barely got the words out before crashing into my father's arms, crying like a defenseless child.

I felt helpless. All these years, this woman took care of me and there was nothing I could do to save her. I had to sit back and accept that she was going to die. God had given me an alcoholic mother but in return I had the best grandmother. Now he decided to take her away. She deserved to live a long life. Seventy-seven was still young. These days people were living way past ninety. I pulled away from my father and wiped my face with my sleeve.

"I hope there's a Heaven, Dad. If I have to let her go, she better be on her way to a magical place."

I wished there was some way of knowing for sure that there was a Heaven. It would make grief a little easier on people if they knew that saying goodbye wasn't permanent. I knew faith played a big role here but what happens when it becomes torn? I walked over to my Auntie Sharon and gave her a hug. She reminded me a lot of my grandmother. I felt her pain through our embrace. All we could do was mourn.

"I'm so sorry, Auntie Sharon."

"I can't believe I am losing my mother." Her words barely made it out of her mouth. Her husband, my Uncle Tony, came over to comfort her. He usually wasn't the affectionate type but he tried. He had been away the day before at a conference in North Carolina and couldn't catch a flight home so he drove all night to be with her.

I then walked over to my Aunt Vivian, who had just hung up the phone. She had called to inform her son Jake about Nanny. Jake was away at college in upstate New York. He was more of a "party animal" and did more drinking than studying. My Aunt Vivian and Uncle Scott had given him a final warning about having too much fun up at school. He had failed two classes and if he didn't change, they were going to make him withdraw.

"I'm so sorry, Aunt Viv," I said as I gave her a hug.

"These things happen, Anna. All we can do now is stick together," she replied.

"Nanny would want that," I agreed.

CHAPTER THREE

I had never lost anyone so close to me before. My mom's father passed away when I was eleven but that was a long time ago. Since then, I haven't had to deal with loss. I guess that made me sort of lucky in a way. I just wished it wasn't my grandmother who was dying. I couldn't eat and wanted to spend as much time with her as I possibly could. I kept going into her room and talking about the times we shared together.

When I first got my driver's license, I had bought a little convertible car. I couldn't wait to take Nanny for a ride in it. She always worried about her hair getting messed up so she made sure she had a little scarf over her head. We went out for ice cream and she had spilt a little chocolate syrup on her skirt. She said, "Not to worry, messes can sometimes build character, so make sure you spill a lot of chocolate syrup in life." That was her way of telling me that it was okay to make mistakes.

All the days I spent with her were great. I felt blessed that she was in my life for twenty-three years but I still wanted more time.

About a year ago, the family was arguing over my grandparent's will. They bickered about land, property, their bank accounts, and even jewelry. As the saying goes, "more money equals more problems." My grandmother started getting upset about it. She turned to me and said, "Everyone else is claiming things they want, so what would you like, Anna?" I will never forget the way I answered her. I said, "When you leave here and go into Heaven, I want you to be my angel. If I am having a bad day or the best day, I want you to be a part of it. That would be the best thing you can give to me." I never realized that day would come so soon. I found myself staring up at the clock, counting down the hours, the minutes, and the seconds I would have left with my grandmother.

As children, we want time to fly because we are anxious to grow up. Once we grow up and realize all the responsibilities and crap we have to deal with, we want to be five again. We often take time for granted. And now, I find myself on the eleventh floor of a hospital waiting room, knowing someone I love is going to die.

"Are you hungry Anna?" my dad asked.

"No, I can't eat," I replied.

"I know it's hard, Anna, but I don't want you to make yourself sick."

"I won't, Dad. I just don't feel like eating right now."

I appreciated my father worrying about me the way a mother should. My mother said she would be coming to the hospital but it was already lunchtime and there was no sign of her. When we went to counseling a few years back, the therapist said, "It's not that she chooses the liquor over her family, it's an illness." It was an illness that I was getting tired of treating without seeing any healthy changes.

Ben was standing up against the wall, making small talk with his father. My grandfather was sitting in a chair talking to my grandmother's brother, who had recently arrived. Distant cousins were there for moral support.

Even though the room was full of family, it still felt so empty. My grandmother was always the light that shined in a room. Parties would never start until she arrived. I knew it would forever be different without her. The hours passed and it was getting late. At 10:30 p.m., the nurse came in and said it wouldn't be long now. Her body was giving up.

The hospital allowed our immediate family to proceed into the room. Poppy took a seat right next to the bed. My father stood behind him with his hands on Poppy's shoulders. The rest of us gathered all around her. Auntie Sharon whispered in her ear, telling her how much she loved her. I was holding onto her hand and laid my head on her chest. I could vaguely hear her heartbeat. Her leg would twitch every now and then. I assumed it was her way of telling us she could hear our words. The nurse said all the patients twitch like that but I wanted to believe it was her way of communicating with us.

My Aunt Vivian thought it would be a good idea to say the "Our Father." As we began praying together, I could barely recite the words. I didn't want to let her go. This was the end. She was really going to die.

Her breathing became less harsh through those damn tubes and I knew she was going to let go soon. The nurse explained what would happen when she passed away. She said that each organ stops working from the inside out and that her hands and body would grow cold after she had passed. All I could think of was her father. He passed away when she was only nine. She lived in Indiana at the time but after he passed away her family moved to Connecticut. My grandmother never got over his death and would cry when she spoke of him. She used to talk about a tire swing she had in her front yard. She would swing on it as she waited for her father to come home from work.

As I laid there watching her slowly leave this world, I imagined her as a little girl, swinging on that tire swing. I hoped if there was a Heaven that her father was right there waiting for her so she wouldn't be afraid.

And just like that, it was over. Her last breath was taken. The time was 11:01 p.m., and she was gone. Perhaps she ascended into Heaven or to a better place, but she was no longer ours. We sat there and cried and comforted one another the best way we could. Ben took it pretty hard. His hug was stronger than any I had ever gotten from him before. We cried enough tears to fill a river.

I didn't want to leave her side. Her hand turned from warm to cold and I felt helpless once again. I had to walk out of the hospital and leave behind the best person I ever knew.

* * *

I gazed out of the car window on the way home. My father was trying to be a strong man but he would sniffle every now and then. He was good at hiding his feelings. I guess most guys were. I put my hand over my father's and said, "Dad, it's going to be okay." He looked over at me and replied, "I know, sweetheart."

In all honesty, I really didn't believe my own words, but someone had to comfort my poor dad.

CHAPTER FOUR

My grandmother's wake was held last night. When our family first arrived, there were lots of tears and sadness. I was surprised at how strong I was during the service. There were lines of people waiting to pay their respects and I greeted all of them with a smile. At the end of the night, my Aunt Sharon told me that my grandmother would have been proud of me.

I knew the funeral would be the hardest part. It was the final good-bye. Although it was late winter, the sun was shining and the temperature was warmer than usual. I had put on my black pencil skirt and a purple pinstriped blouse. Purple was her favorite color so I wanted to make sure I wore it. I threw on a black blazer to look more presentable and put my hair in a low ponytail. I dabbed on some powder and applied a neutral-colored lip gloss. I chose not to use mascara. I didn't want to look like a raccoon once the tears started to fall. My eyes were still burning from all the crying last night. I put two small sprays of perfume on my neck and was ready to go. I wanted this day to be over.

My mother was going with us to the funeral. I was surprised she decided to put away her booze for the day and act like a wife and mother. She came up with all kinds of excuses for why she didn't stay longer at the hospital. Of course, my dad let it go. I think he didn't have the energy to argue with her.

Not one word was spoken on our way to the church in my dad's Beemer. I looked over the reading that I volunteered for. I felt nervous that I wouldn't be able to get the words out but I knew I had to try. I wanted to honor my grandmother.

"How Great Thou Art" was the song playing as we followed the casket into the church. When I heard that song, my insides started to crumble. The tears raced out and I wasn't going to try and stop them. I could barely see to walk. The pain in my heart was unbearable.

I took a seat in the pew and my dad passed me a tissue. As the song continued to play, I thought about its message. The words described how great God was and how we need to acknowledge all the beautiful moments in life, things like the rolling thunder and the gentle breeze. Our lives tend to be so rushed that we often forget to slow down and enjoy those natural gifts.

My mother, of all people, put her arm around me. She was trying to be comforting. I couldn't help but wonder if it was sincere. Was she just trying to act like a good mother in front of the family? Either way, at that moment, I let her console me. It wasn't nearly as comforting as my grandmother's hugs, but I don't think anything will ever come close to that.

The priest, Father Bob, began to talk about my grandmother and all the things she did for the church and for her family. He kept saying we were celebrating her life but I wasn't in any mood to celebrate. He spoke of her community involvement with the Girl Scouts and how she was always donating money to those less fortunate. Father Bob said she was one of the good ones and that Heaven holds a special place for her. My grandmother liked him. He even shed some tears as he was talking about her. She really did affect so many people in ways I don't think I ever could. She certainly was an angel that had earned her wings.

Ben walked up to the podium to do the first reading. He was dressed in a nice navy blue suit. His hair was properly combed and he spoke with such poise.

I gazed down at my own reading and kept trying to pronounce the word "Ecclesiastes." I really hoped I wouldn't mess this up too bad, especially having to follow Ben's superb job. I wanted this day to be perfect for her. Father Bob called my name for the second reading and my heart began to palpitate. Public speaking was not my forté. I adjusted the microphone and began. I tried to read every word with proper enunciation so it didn't sound mumbled.

"And this is a reading from the book of Ecclesiastes," I said with great relief.

I was so glad when that was over. As I sat back down in the pew, I stared over at the casket. My grandmother was lying inside of that mahogany box. She would have no more breaths, no more smiles, and no more voice to sing. I wondered if she was in the church watching her own funeral. A part of me didn't want her to see our sorrows but at the same time, I wanted her to know how much we were going to miss her.

I peered down to see my grandpa who was sitting with a blank stare. My Aunt Sharon comforted him but like my dad, he barely showed any emotion. I knew his heart was full of pain and there was no Band-aid big enough to stop his bleeding. My grandmother took care of him. She cooked for him and did all the bookkeeping for his pallet business. I don't think the man even knew how to boil water. Who would take care of him now?

I looked behind me and saw Chelsea and Ryan. They have been my best friends since kindergarten. They were sitting with their families, watching the service. I was glad to have them in my life. Chelsea only had one grandparent. It was her mother's father. The other three had passed away before she was even born. Her grandfather had all kinds of health issues, though. They visited him sometimes at the convalescent home but they weren't very close. I wondered if my family would ever put my grandpa in one of those dreadful places.

The pallbearers walked out of the pews as the Mass had ended. We followed behind them. Extended family members and friends tried to comfort us as we walked by. I had a hard time even looking up at them as I felt numerous hands caress my backside. The only arms I wanted around me were the arms that no longer existed.

* * *

The cemetery was just as I expected. It was somber and the tears continued to fall. I raised my face to the sky and let the sun's rays beam down on me. It felt warm on my skin and a gentle breeze blew through my hair that gave me a little chill. I heard a saying once that love is like a breeze, you can't see it, but you feel it. That was it. Even though I could no longer see her, maybe she was still there. When I looked down at her casket, it looked like a translucent purplish color. I couldn't believe that I actually thought a casket looked beautiful, but I knew the person inside of it was. I walked over to it and took a rose from the bouquet.

My grandmother was notorious for collecting a rose at every funeral she attended. She would then press it onto a page in her Bible. I decided I would do the same thing, although I had hoped I wouldn't be attending any more funerals for awhile.

The service ended and it felt bittersweet. I still wasn't ready to leave my grandmother. People started saying their good-byes. My stomach started to rumble and I felt famished. Family and friends headed over to Carmelo's for lunch. It was a banquet hall my family booked because they knew the owners.

We ate a nice meal at Carmelo's and shared stories about my grandmother. There was even some laughter in the room. I kept thinking that she would walk in at any moment but of course she didn't. From that moment on, she would only be there in our hearts.

"I'm stuffed," Ryan said as he threw down his napkin.

"The food was very good," Chelsea replied.

"Thanks, guys, for coming. I really appreciate you being here," I said to them.

"Anna, of course we would be here for you. Your grandmother was a great lady, and Chelsea and I both considered her family," explained Ryan.

"We really did, Anna. And you know I never really had any grandparents, so I was glad to share yours," Chelsea added.

"Awe, guys, she really thought the world of the both of you, too. I still can't believe she's gone," I said.

"She's not Anna," Chelsea said as she put her hand over mine. "She's a part of you and you're a part of her. That will never change."

I guess sometimes people do know the right words to say in these situations. I had my grandmother's long fingers and her hearty laugh. Most importantly, I had her love, and that lasts forever.

"Anna, if you need us for anything, you know you can ask," said

Ryan as he got up to throw away his plate.

He was a great friend. Ryan seemed to have bad luck with the girls but that was only because he was too nice. Someday he would find a good woman.

After the banquet hall, the immediate family gathered over Aunt Vivian's house. Her house was huge and set up more like a museum. Everything had its proper place and even the cherry wood trim was glimmering. There was more food there. She went above and beyond with the spread. She had everything from pasta to shrimp and even salads. Some people referred to her as being overly "showy." Status meant a lot to her and I think she got some of that from my Uncle Scott. He was born into an extremely wealthy family and my Aunt Viv only wanted to impress her in-laws.

My Auntie Sharon was the opposite. She was more laid-back and could care less if a few dust bunnies were under her couch. In fact, she was a lot like my grandmother. She would rather spend her time with those she loved than worry about what her house looked like.

My father was a mix of Aunt Vivian and Auntie Sharon. He was the spoiled child growing up. I always heard stories about how my dad always got his way and could have anything he wanted. I guess karma eventually caught up because his sisters definitely won the better spouses. Speaking of spouses, I noticed my mom getting into Aunt Vivian's whiskey. She was pouring one glass after another. I had wished Aunt Vivian left her liquor cabinet locked up. It was sad that she couldn't go one day without alcohol.

Ryan and Chelsea both stopped over my aunt's for a bit. They wanted to make sure I was okay. "Anna, we have to leave for work but call us later if you need anything," said Chelsea. I hugged them both and said, "Thanks again for coming."

Ryan and Chelsea worked at Harvey's. It was a small grocery store in town. For years they had been trying to get me to work with them but I was happy where I was. I worked at a little café/bookshop and I could study and do homework when we didn't have customers. I also liked reading those self-help books. Sometimes they assisted me with my own case studies for my psych classes. I didn't always see the "help" in them but some people do; otherwise, we would not sell them.

I decided to go outside and sit on the porch swing. I needed some fresh air. The peace and quiet was nice too. There were a lot of stars out and I could see my breath as I exhaled in the cold night's air. "I sure hope you made it to Heaven safely," I said as I looked up to the sky.

I thought about a song my grandmother used to sing to me while rocking me to sleep. Instead of singing "Daddy's Little Girl," she changed the words to "Nanny's Little Girl." I wished I could hear her sing it to me one last time.

Once again, my eyes began to rain. I heard the front door open and out came my Auntie Sharon. She took a seat next to me on the swing and asked me if I was alright. For everything she had been through with her mother, she was doing great. I knew it would only be a matter of time before she exploded with tears but for now she was managing pretty well.

"The day's almost over," she said.

"I still can't believe she is gone. It seems like she's on a vacation or something," I said wiping my tears.

"I hope she is and that it's someplace really beautiful and peaceful, like she deserves," Auntie Sharon replied.

"She definitely deserves the best of everything," I said.

We sat there for another ten minutes, not saying a word, but somehow we felt comforted.

CHAPTER FIVE

Downstairs, I heard my father raise his voice at my mother.

"One day, damn it! One goddamn day! You couldn't refrain from a lick of alcohol. It was my mother's funeral."

I walked out of my room and down a few stairs to listen. It had been awhile since my father scolded my mother, mainly because she was always intoxicated and it didn't help anything.

"I'm done. I cannot handle this habit of yours anymore. Don't come back in this house unless you want to get help."

The door slammed and out she went. Once again, I felt helpless. I was studying to be a psychologist but there was no helping her. A person with an addiction cannot be helped until they want to change. My mother was not ready. I started to think she never would be.

I made my way back up the stairs. I wanted to check on my father but I figured he needed some time alone. His plate was full of chaos, between losing his mother and dealing with my mom's addiction. I'm not sure how he was able to keep it all together. I crawled into my bed and went to sleep. Thank God the weekend was here. I was not prepared to go back to school and needed the weekend to rejuvenate. I was feeling crappy so I stayed in bed till 11:30.

My mom never came home. My father was out in the garage keeping his mind occupied. After I dragged myself out of bed, I decided to take a drive to the shore. The ocean air always had a calming effect. It was only forty degrees outside but that didn't stop me. I threw on a sweatshirt and got into my car. I brought a pair of gloves and a blanket. There wasn't a soul in sight. I was completely alone and I liked it.

As I looked out over the horizon, I wondered if my grandmother was happy. If only there was a way she could send me a sign so I would know she was alright. A few birds were flying overhead. They looked so free. I laid down on my blanket and watched them soar.

People always seem to look up at the sky when a loved one passes on. I assumed it was because they felt that their loved ones were now angels and could fly. I wondered if my grandmother was an angel now with wings. How would I ever know...in fact, what if there was no Heaven? What if someone made it all up so that the pain wouldn't be as bad when we lose someone we love? I hated even thinking like that. All the scientific research shows and books made me second-guess God, Jesus, the Bible, and even Heaven. I've read that the Bible was written by Constantine and that he only included what he wanted. Researchers had also discovered other ancient writings that go against what is in the Bible. Could Heaven really exist? It all seemed like a magical fairy tale. There wasn't any proof that I'd ever witnessed anyway. I started to get angry and upset. The tears once again began to drown me. I couldn't bear to think that my grandmother was just gone and not in some beautiful place. She deserved the idea of Heaven and all that went with it.

I felt someone touch my shoulder. I jumped and noticed it was Chelsea.

"Your dad told me I would find you here," she said as she sat beside me. I wiped my tears and she tried comforting me. "I wish I could make it better for you," she said.

"You do, Chels, I'm so glad to see you. I just can't stop thinking... what if there is no Heaven?" Chelsea was the best person to help me through this. She was very spiritual.

"Of course there's a Heaven, Anna. This life is not the end for us," she preached.

"How do you know, though?" I questioned her certainty.

"Faith," she replied.

One simple answer, yet I felt I was losing my faith. Would I ever get it back?

"Anna, it's normal to have these feelings and question your faith when a loved one passes away. When my cousin died, my aunt asked the pastor why she felt so lost when death should bring her closer to God. He told her it was because she was normal. Some people become closer to God or their religion when a loved one passes away and others, like you, start to question it. Your faith will come back. It just takes time," Chelsea explained as she put her arm around my shoulder.

"I hate feeling like this. I went to church with her every Sunday and now here I am, feeling confused," I said.

"God gave us hearts to love, hands to hold, fingers to touch, and so many wonderful things. Think of how a baby is created. You mean to tell me that nasty bodily fluid from a man mixed with a woman transforms into a life?" she questioned.

"Well, yes, Chels, didn't you listen in Health Education?" I asked with a sarcastic laugh.

"You can't possibly believe that a life is given just based on fluids. It has to be from love, from some type of miracle," Chelsea explained passionately.

"What if I believe and then I die and there is nothing?" I asked.

"Then it is what you just said. It is nothing and you won't know any damn difference," she laughed.

Chelsea and I sat and talked for awhile as we enjoyed the empty beach. Our noses were cold, our bums sat on the frigid sand, and our teeth chattered, but we didn't seem to mind. As the sun went down, it grew colder.

"I love how the moon shines over the ocean, and makes the water look like little diamonds sparkling throughout," I said.

"It's just another one of God's gifts of nature, Anna," she replied with a smile.

"I dread what my family will be like now."

Chelsea looked confused. "What do you mean?" she asked.

"My grandmother always kept everyone together. She was the head of our family and without her I have a feeling things may get heated."

"Nah, you have such a close family, Anna, I'm sure everyone will be supportive. You all may even grow closer as you mourn her loss."

I hoped she was right but I knew how my family would be. Whenever there were riches involved, problems usually followed. "I hope so, Chels, but you know people always get greedy and I'm just worried about the family arguing over money."

"Well, your grandpa is still alive and he needs to survive so you won't have to worry about any of that until he passes away," Chelsea said.

"Yeah, you're probably right," I replied as I stood up and wiped the sand off my jeans. "We should go. I'm freezing and kind of hungry."

Chelsea helped me fold up my blanket and then she threw her arms around me. "Everything is going to be fine," she said.

I was lucky to have a best friend like Chelsea. Sometimes friends were more meaningful to us than our own families. As we got back into our cars to drive home, I took one more look out at the waves crashing down on the ocean floor. I tried to somehow feel spiritual but nothing was happening. Perhaps Chelsea was right. I just needed some time.

* * *

Later that night when I got home, I started studying for an upcoming exam. A call came through from my Auntie Sharon.

"Hello," I said.

"Can I just tell you how sick of this family I am? Your Aunt Vivian is a real piece of work," she began to ramble on about how horrible my aunt was acting.

My two aunts had an atrocious relationship. They were never close, even as children, but I never knew how bad it really was. Aunt Sharon went on for a good five minutes about how my Aunt Vivian was trying to get my grandfather to read my grandmother's will.

"I thought you didn't read anyone's will until both spouses have passed." I said.

"You would think so, but my jerk of a sister wants to get it done and over with. They went to the lawyer's office today," she said angrily.

"Already? That does seem overly ambitious. How does Poppy feel about all that? I mean, he just lost his wife." I asked.

"Exactly, let the man mourn and not have to deal with all the hassle of the will," said Aunt Sharon.

She did share a lot of valid points. Why would Aunt Vivian be so superficial in wanting the will read when my grandmother hadn't even been gone a week? That was her personality though, always thinking business. My father was no angel but I doubt he was thinking about the will. Shortly after I hung up with Aunt Sharon, he was calling me down for dinner.

Eating dinner with my family lately was uncomfortable. We barely spoke and when we did, it seemed scripted. Mom had returned home after my father cooled down about her drinking. It was a vicious cycle. I wish he had stuck more to his guns about her getting help, but I know he didn't want her on the streets. For some reason, I felt the need to tell them about my conversation with Aunt Sharon.

"I had an interesting talk with Aunt Sharon about Nanny's will," I said.

My dad took a deep breath. It seemed as if he wasn't happy she told me about it. "And what did my sister have to say?" he asked.

"Just that Aunt Vivian is pressuring Poppy to read her will and how she doesn't agree with it. Do you think they should read it, Dad?" I asked.

He put his napkin down. "I don't know, Anna. I don't think you should be getting involved in these types of conversations, though."

"I see. So, is it because you don't think I can handle it, or because you don't want me involved with the family business?" I asked.

"Both. You need to focus on school right now," he replied.

I looked down at my plate and then over at my mother who sat there like a statue.

"She was my grandmother, Dad, and she was very much like a mother to me…and I agree with Aunt Sharon. We all need to mourn right now and not be concerned with material things," I tried explaining.

My mother turned to me and said, "Well, I'm sorry, Anna, that you lost your *real* mother but like your father said, it's best to stay out of family affairs."

I looked at my mother with disgust. "Yeah Mom, like the way I need to stay out of your booze addiction issues. You have no idea how it is to live here. You are right about one thing…I did lose my real mother."

"Anna! That is enough!" my father shouted.

"I just lost my appetite," I said as I left the table and went up to my room.

I could hear my mother and father yelling at each other downstairs. I know I caused the argument but I was so tired of sitting back and letting all those horrible things happen. I've closed my eyes long enough and I am not blind to the problems we face as a family. Sometimes I wish I had gone away to college. Then again, I wouldn't have had all that time with my grandmother. As I was now learning, time doesn't stop and we certainly cannot rewind it.

I felt guilty yelling at my mom and treating her that way, but what about all the times she didn't act like a mother? My parents went on yelling for about twenty minutes before she finally walked out and slammed the door. My guess is she was going out drinking again. I couldn't understand how or why he continued to put up with her. He must have really taken his vows seriously because he couldn't possibly be happy with her.

I probably shouldn't have chewed out my mother, especially since my father was also still mourning. My dad really had no one to turn to. He had friends but men tend to do things like go golfing with their buddies, not talk about things or gossip. Now I wished I never told my parents about Aunt Sharon's call.

* * *

The next morning, I found my father sitting at the kitchen table. He wasn't drinking his coffee or reading the paper. He was just looking out of the window as if he was in deep thought. I took out a bowl and poured myself some cereal. I sat down beside him and decided to apologize.

"Dad, I'm really sorry about last night. I know you just lost grandma too and you're dealing with mom at the same time. I had no right to say anything."

He looked up at me with a smile and said, "Anna, I know how this is affecting you too. I have to protect my little girl the best I can. At this point, you're all I have that is normal. I don't want you to get involved with all the family mumbo jumbo."

"Mumbo jumbo, Dad, really?" We both laughed.

"Hey Dad, I need to print out my final thesis for my forensics class and our printer is out of ink. I was going to go and use Poppy's later if you think that's okay?" I asked.

"Sure sweetie. Aunt Vivian actually called a family meeting over there tonight so you can ride with me if you'd like. I'm leaving around seven," he said.

"Perfect Dad, thanks," I said as I put my empty bowl into the sink and grabbed my backpack for school. "I'm running late this morning so I will see you later then."

"Okay, have a great day Anna," Dad said.

As I walked out and closed the door behind me, I stood there for a minute looking in at him sitting at the table. My heart grew heavy as I felt bad for him. I got in my car and drove off.

* * *

I ran into Chelsea in the student lounge. She was studying to be a marketing professional. It suited her well as she was so good with people.

"So my Aunt Vivian wants a family meeting tonight," I said to her.

"A family meeting for what?" she asked.

"My guess is to talk about my grandmother's will."

"I thought they normally talk about a will when both people pass on?"

"Yep, that's what I thought too, but apparently my Aunt Viv went to a lawyer with my Poppy and already discussed the details."

"Wow, she has some balls, eh?" Chelsea commented. (I love how blunt Chelsea can be sometimes). "Well, good luck, Anna. It'll get easier," she said.

"I hope so," I replied as I scooted off to the Psychology building. I was having a hard time concentrating in class. That was unusual, seeing it was the most interesting class I've taken during my entire college career. The class was called Human Sexuality, and the teacher was a bit fruity.

I stared down at my desk, wondering what my grandmother was thinking about all of this family drama. Was she disappointed or was she even aware? I had hoped she wasn't watching because she'd probably be hurt that instead of mourning, we were already fighting. Just then, I heard the professor call on me, "Miss Corolla, what do you think about the conflicting opinions over size? Does it matter?" I swallowed a chicken, or at least it felt like I did. *Did she just seriously ask me what I thought about the male penis size?*

"Uh," I stuttered as I could feel everyone's eyes glued on me.

"Come on now, it's an open-minded class, so tell us your opinion, unless of course you have never actually seen one?"

Did she really just say that?

I laughed with huge embarrassment and said, "I prefer average myself, although I think it has more to do with talent when you utilize it."

She seemed impressed as she replied, "My dear, what a stellar answer."

This woman should have been a porn star, not a college professor. She kept going on and on about the male size and all the different proportions. I wondered where she stood with faith. She probably assumed that Heaven was some big orgy or she was probably hoping it was.

I had a quick dinner at the deli with Chelsea and Ryan. I told them all about my sex question in class. They both laughed so hard that Ryan spit out a mouthful of coffee.

"I can't believe you told her you preferred average penises," Chelsea laughed.

"What's wrong with average penises?" asked Ryan.

"Nothing, if you had one," Chelsea sarcastically replied.

"I have an average seven incher," he replied.

"Okay guys, can we please stop talking about penis sizes?" I asked.

"Well, you haven't seen one in awhile, Anna," Chelsea said.

"I know a guy," said Ryan.

"Guys, I don't need to get laid, okay? I can find a penis all by myself. With school and everything going on, I just don't have time for penis…I mean *men*, right now," I said with a laugh.

"You're still broken up from Carl, aren't you?" Chelsea asked.

"No, no, it has nothing to do with him," I said.

"Are you sure? I know you weren't happy when he chose to move to the city?" Ryan said.

"His music is important to him and we're young. Of course he should choose his dream over some girl," I explained.

"But you're not just some girl, Anna. You are someone he should never have let go," Chelsea said.

"He's doing great in New York. I had to let him go, otherwise, he would have resented me for it," I explained.

"I think you're afraid to let someone new in, Anna," explained Chelsea.

"It's not that. I just haven't met anyone worth my time."

"What is it with women and musicians?" asked Ryan.

"It's not just musicians, Ry. We connected both mentally and physically. It's hard to find that combo and I'm not going to rush into bed with some frat boy when I know there is something better out there waiting for me," I explained.

"Just don't wait too long, Anna. You wouldn't want to have to dust yourself off," Chelsea joked.

"Very funny. Let's stop talking about my sex life now, okay?" I exclaimed. "I better start heading home. I don't want to be late for this big family meeting."

"Have fun with that," said Ryan.

"Call me later if the meeting turns into World War Four," Chelsea said.

"I will, thanks guys," I said as I walked out to my car.

I was nervous about the meeting at my grandfather's house. I hated seeing my family argue the way they had been lately. I had hoped that somehow they would be cordial with each other tonight.

* * *

When I got home my dad asked me about school. I didn't dare share with him the extreme embarrassment I experienced in class. He could tell something was bothering me. My dad always worked his power of persuasion to get me to talk.

"What are your thoughts on Heaven, Dad?" I asked. He was quiet for a moment and then just said, "I believe there is a Heaven."

"I just started thinking today about Heaven and God and if the two even exist," I explained. He looked over at me and said, "Anna, I think most people have doubts."

"I know people mourn in different ways but I hate that I'm in doubt about my faith when it was Nanny who took me to church every Sunday," I replied.

"Anna, you were raised to have faith and a belief in the afterlife. Don't question it because the truth is, no one really knows what happens after we die. That's why it's called faith," he said.

"I took a Philosophy class once and I believe it was Socrates who said, 'Death can be either two things. It's either a constant state of nothingness or it is a relocation of the soul from earth to another place.' So basically, we shouldn't fear it because it's either everything we hope it to be or it's like nights where we don't dream," I explained.

"Sounds like you just answered your own question," my father replied.

As we pulled into my grandfather's driveway, a feeling of sadness filled my stomach. Lately, when I visit, I have a hard time accepting that my grandmother is not sitting in her usual chair. The last conversation we ever had was outside in her driveway. I never thought in a million years that would be the last time I would ever speak with her. I keep reliving that moment and how I wish I ran to her and gave her one last squeeze. It hasn't even been a month and I already missed her hugs. I know they say laughter is the best medicine but not for me, it was her hugs that made me better.

We walked into the kitchen and everyone was sitting down. Poppy was sitting at the head of the table and both Aunt Vivian and Auntie Sharon were mute. The mood was intense and I just wanted to go to the office where I could be alone.

Aunt Vivian was sipping on some tea with a folder in front of her, while Aunt Sharon sat and stared off like she was already disgusted. My dad took a seat between Aunt Vivian and Aunt Sharon. I guess he was going to be playing the role of mediator.

I walked over to my grandfather, kissed him on the forehead, and said hello. Aunt Sharon stood up to give me a hug and then I went over to Aunt Vivian and gave her one as well. I grabbed a quick drink of water and then made my way down the hall to the office. I felt relieved to be out of that kitchen. It used to be the place where I'd enjoy having conversations with my grandmother or learn how to bake her famous lasagna. Now it was a room full of tension.

I plugged my laptop into the printer and pulled up my thesis. At first, the house was pretty quiet but after awhile I could hear the discussion getting heated. I wanted to open the door so I could hear what was going on but I was already depressed. Instead, I focused on my work. As the paper slid out of the printer, I looked for a stapler. I rustled through the drawers and came across some old mail my grandmother must have stuck in there for some reason—things like old store flyers and junk mail ads for election time. I started to put them back when I noticed an envelope stuck to the back of one of the flyers. I pulled it off and saw it was a letter addressed to my grandmother from someone in Indiana. It had a pretty flower sticker on the front to seal it. It was dated September 14, 2009, which was only a few months ago. A part of me wanted to open it but another part of me felt like I was invading her personal space. I heard someone walking down the hallway so I quickly put the envelope into my laptop bag.

"Hey kiddo, are you almost ready to go?" It was my father. The big meeting must have come to a close.

"Sure Dad, I'm just going to staple my work and we can head home," I said.

"Okay, I'll meet you out at the car then," he responded as he walked out of the room.

I found the stapler, put my paper in a folder, and then into my bag. I shut down my laptop and turned off the printer. When I walked back into the kitchen, I noticed Aunt Sharon was already gone and Aunt Vivian was on the phone with someone.

"Goodnight Poppy," I said as I leaned over to give him a hug good-bye.

"Did you finish what you needed for your paper?" he asked.

"I did. Thank you so much for allowing me to use the printer," I answered.

"Anytime, Anna," he replied.

I bet he was having a hard time living in that house without my grandmother. My aunts and my father tried their best to keep him company but they could never fill that void of my grandmother's presence.

The car ride home was quiet. I wanted to ask my dad how it went but then I remembered how he didn't want me involved in the family drama.

"Your mother is going to check into a rehab center," my father blurted out. I was definitely not expecting to hear those words come out of his mouth. "Really? For how long?" I questioned.

"Forty-five days. It's a place up in Vermont that was highly recommended," he replied.

"By who?" I asked with much curiosity. "The Internet," he explained.

"I guess that's good, but from what I know, people only get better when they are ready to. Do you really think Mom is ready?"

He took a deep breath and said, "Anna, I told her if she didn't get the help, then our marriage was over. You are almost twenty-two years old. Soon you will have a career and may start a family of your own. I figured it was time to make a stand."

I looked down at my fiddling hands and said, "It's about time, Dad. I'm glad you finally agreed to put your happiness first. I know you have been dealing with Mom's issues mainly so we could stay a family, but what kind of family have we really been?"

For the second time in my life, I saw a tear fall from my father's eyes. He cleared his throat as he was looking for the right words to say to me.

"Anna, I know it has been very hard on you, between your mother's bad habit and losing Grandma. You turned out to be one amazing woman and I'm so proud to be your father. Even though your grandmother cannot be there at your graduation, she'll be there in spirit. I don't think even Heaven will stop her from watching you walk across that stage," he said with a laugh.

My father has never till this moment really told me how proud he was of me. I'd get the occasional "great job" or "way to go," but for him to really dig deep and say those words to me meant something special. I grabbed hold of his hand and squeezed it.

"Thank you for being the best dad a girl could ever ask for," I said.

He just smiled at me and held my hand.

CHAPTER SIX

"To graduation, and leaving behind all those late nights of caffeine and writing papers," Chelsea said as she raised her shot glass up high in the air.

"I'll toast to that," I said as I clinked my glass against hers.

"You girls and your Patron," Ryan said.

"Oh shut up, you wannabe-Irishman drinking Guinness," laughed Chelsea.

"Yes, but tomorrow morning while you girls are hungover, I will be ready to walk across that stage," he said.

"Oh and I suppose beer doesn't cause hangovers?" I asked.

"Beer before liquor get sicker, and liquor before beer you shall have no fear. Since I already drank a couple of vodka tonics, I will be good now switching to beer," said the ever-so-intelligent Ryan.

"You are going to do great things in life, Ry," I said as I gave him a squeeze.

"And you, Anna, will listen to all the world's problems and fix them. You will be like the modern day Gandhi," he said. "I seriously doubt that but I shall try," I said.

"And you, Chelsea, will move to the Big Apple and get some fancy corporate job, marry a Wall Street guy, and have two babies," Ryan said as he took a huge gulp of his beer.

"I didn't know you were a psychic. Maybe you can now tell me what the Powerball numbers are for tonight's drawing," Chelsea said as she downed another shot of tequila.

"You may want to go easy on those shots, Chels," I said.

"Don't you worry, Anna, I have the perfect hangover prevention tool," she replied.

"And what's that?" asked Ryan.

"Just drink more in the morning," she said with slurred drunken words.

"Or you could try Ibuprofen with water," I said.

Tomorrow was graduation day for Chelsea, Ryan, and I—the day we dreamed about since we were twelve. We used to sit under an old apple tree and talk about what we would be when we grew up. Ryan always said he was going to be an FBI agent because he thought it would attract girls. Instead, he is getting his MBA and will be working as an actuarial assistant for some insurance company in Hartford. Chelsea landed a job at The Mullen Group which is New York City's finest marketing firm. She has always wanted to live in a big city and New York isn't too far away. As for me, I have no idea what I am going to do. I got an offer from an emergency hotline company out of Boston for people who are suicidal, but I'm just not sure that's the route I want to take. Something will come up, I'm sure.

"So when are you going to take your big trip, Anna?" Ryan asked as he let out a huge burp.

"My big trip?" I asked with utmost confusion.

"Yeah, don't you remember last year when you said after graduation you would take some exotic vacation? I think it was Bali or Abu Dhabi maybe," he replied.

I laughed and said, "Well, I need money for that trip so I guess my next adventure will really be to find a job."

Chelsea chimed in with her drunkenness and said, "Yes, but tonight we are celebrating so let's dance!" She swayed over to the jukebox in the corner.

"She is so going to be sorry in the morning," I said to Ryan. He laughed. "Amen to that, sister."

Chelsea came over and grabbed us to dance with her. As we were dancing around like a bunch of drunken college kids, I knew this was the beginning of the rest of our lives. For the first time in quite awhile, I was smiling and laughing. We were the only ones dancing in that bar but we didn't care. I needed this night. Chelsea stopped us for a moment and said, "Promise me that we will never go such a long time again without talking or seeing each other?" Ryan and I both said at the same time, "We promise." We then embraced each other in a group hug and knew we had to get home to prepare for our big day.

* * *

The next morning I felt nervous. Maybe I was fearful that I would fall down on the stage just as I was receiving my degree. Or maybe my body was still full of alcohol from the night before.

I wore a yellow spring dress I had bought at the mall a few weeks ago specifically for this day. I opened my jewelry box and took out the lavaliere necklace my grandmother had bought me for my eighteenth birthday. I wanted her to somehow be a part of this day even though physically she couldn't. As I looked in the mirror, I realized I was ready. My dad walked in with Aunt Sharon.

"Aunt Sharon, you're here?" I said happily.

"I wouldn't miss my Godchild's graduation for the world. Now here, put on your cap and gown so I can get a few pictures," she said.

I was glad Aunt Sharon was there since my mom couldn't make it. I understood why she wasn't there but it still hurt. I tried to shake it off as this was my day and nothing was going to ruin it.

"Okay, Frankie, get with your daughter," Aunt Sharon ordered Dad to pose for a picture with me.

My dad looked down at me with a smile and said, "You look like an educated woman ready to face the world. I sure hope they are ready for you."

"Dad, they will never be quite ready for me," I said with a laugh.

"That's my girl," Aunt Sharon piped in. "We better get going as we don't want Anna to be late."

"Thanks again, Auntie Sharon, for being here, it means so much to me." She leaned over and gave me a big hug. It was almost as good as my grandmother's.

"I love you so much, Anna. You've always been like a daughter to me and you really are going to do amazing things in life."

"I love you too, Auntie Sharon."

"Okay, enough with the 'I love you's' already, we really are going to be late," Dad said as he grabbed the keys.

Dad and Aunt Sharon dropped me off in front of the theater where our graduation was to be held. Looking around at all of my fellow classmates dressed in their caps and gowns, snapping pictures and smiling, I knew it would be a great day. I wondered where everyone was headed next. Would they score their dream job or settle down with children and marriage? Would they live here in Connecticut or move away to start anew? The possibilities were endless and it scared me to death. Was I ready for this? I'd soon be finding my own job, moving into my own apartment, and starting my new life. Where would my family fit in? Would we still get together and would it be the same? I started to think about my grandmother and how proud this day would have made her. I felt a little jealous as I saw some students with elderly people I assumed were grandparents. As I started to feel sorry for myself, I felt a tap on my shoulder.

"Ryan, check you out, handsome," I said.

"Yes, I am GQ, what can I say? Miss Corolla, if I didn't know you most of my life, I would be so into you. That cap and gown accents your womanly figure so perfectly," he said as he stared me up and down and gave me a twirl.

"Shut up, you weirdo. Where is Chels?" I asked.

"Haven't seen her. She will probably show up fashionably late as usual," Ryan replied.

"Yeah, and fashionably hungover," I said.

We made our way into the theater where the graduates had to line up. They separated us by areas of study. Ryan was all alone with the rest of the MBA folks and Chelsea and I somehow were lucky enough to have been grouped together. I liked how they allowed us to sit with whoever we pleased in our particular groups. I would never have made it through another long graduation ceremony without Chelsea entertaining me. It's nice to have speeches from successful people who try offering up advice for the future, but sometimes they really go off on a tangent. I remember at my high school graduation one of the speakers started talking about global warming. He totally lost us and Chelsea came to the rescue by handing me a Jolly Rancher. I'm not sure I could have made it through that speech without the sweet taste of watermelon.

I looked into the crowd and saw my dad sitting with Aunt Sharon and Aunt Vivian. I was glad Aunt Vivian came too, even though I felt a little upset with her about the will. It was nice seeing them all sitting together. I'm sure there were still hard feelings between Aunt Sharon and Aunt Vivian. I gave them credit for pushing that issue aside for my graduation ceremony.

My Poppy couldn't come because he hadn't been feeling well. Aunt Sharon thinks it's because of all the bullshit happening in the family related to Grandmother's death. I'd have to agree with her. No one came from my mom's side. She had two brothers but they both live out of state. One of them was in a 70s tribute band that toured around the West coast but I never knew much else about him. The other settled down with a family in Salt Lake City and I've only seen him twice at family weddings.

"This is going to be torture," Chelsea said as I saw her pull something out of her purse.

"Starburst!" I softly shouted.

Chelsea looked at me with a devilish smile. *Oh, how I loved her.* We sat through the speeches while shoving a Starburst in our mouth every few minutes. We tried really hard to not make noise with the wrappers. One of the speeches was by far the best one I have heard at any graduation. It was about a man who started his own business and had great success. He shared his fortune by giving back to the community and built recreational centers for inner city kids. He left us with the most inspirational quote: *"Think about something each day that you know you can't fail at, and then go do it!"*

Quotes can sometimes mean different things to different people. To me, it meant "don't waste time and go after what you want." We sometimes have to try new things in life, even if it scares us. It doesn't mean that we would fail. It just means we have to have enough courage and enthusiasm to do it.

A little while later they called our group up to walk the stage and receive our ticket for the future. I, of course, wore flats because it was the safe choice. Chelsea wore these really cute pumps but she always was the risk taker. I wished I was more like her. Men drop at the sight of her because she is always perfect in every way. Even in a pair of sweatpants with her hair tied back, she looked amazing. Chelsea didn't have to try hard at being beautiful, even though I'm sure she took two hours getting ready this morning.

As I heard my name called over the microphone, my heart was racing. I could feel the blood rushing to my face as I reached to shake hands with the Dean. You would think after a high school graduation and a Bachelors ceremony, I would be a pro at this, but it made me nervous every time. As I came off the stage, Chelsea gave me a huge hug and we stopped so her folks could snap a picture of us with our Masters in hand.

After graduation, my father wanted to treat Aunt Sharon, Aunt Vivian, and I to a nice lunch. We went to a steak house in town that had the best filets. Both Aunt Vivian and Aunt Sharon handed me an envelope with a check inside—my graduation present.

"I know it won't pay off your entire college loan but perhaps it will help make a dent," Aunt Vivian said jokingly.

"I really appreciate it, guys. The gift is really not necessary. It meant a lot to me that you both were there today," I replied.

"You looked so elegant walking across the stage, Anna," said Aunt Sharon.

"I was a nervous wreck," I said with a laugh.

"Stages freak me out too," Aunt Sharon replied.

"No more stages for awhile unless you go for a Doctorate degree," said Aunt Vivian.

"Well, I think I am going to take a break from school for awhile," I said.

"I don't blame you," she agreed.

The rest of the lunch went well. I was a little nervous to see how Aunt Vivian and Aunt Sharon would get along. They were very civil and focused mainly on me and my graduation. I was thankful for that afternoon even though I felt a huge piece missing.

That night, Chelsea made me promise her that I would go to a frat party. During the six years I attended college, I hadn't been to many parties. I focused so much on schoolwork and my job that I barely had time for fun. Tonight would be different. I was going to be young and crazy and maybe even flirt with some of the frat boys.

Ryan and his brother were going too. Ryan's brother didn't drink much so we'd have a designated driver. I never understood why someone would agree to be a designated driver, having to spend all night hanging around with drunks and then driving them home. Everyone else gets to have fun while you watch and babysit. I never drank too much because I saw what it did to my family and how it altered my mother's behavior. Chelsea always thought I was being too precautious and that I would be nothing like my mother. I was still afraid to drink often because I never want to be like her.

"So how does it feel to be done with school?" my father asked as we got into his car after lunch.

"Scary actually," I replied. "I have no idea where I am going to work and it seems like everyone else has a plan."

"Don't worry, sweetie. You will figure things out. And you do know that you can stay at home for as long as you want or need to," he explained.

"Thanks Dad. I appreciate that."

"So, what's your plan for tonight?" he asked.

The one downfall to living at home was that your parents still worried. My dad claims he doesn't still wait up for me but every time I come home late, he is asleep in the chair with the TV on.

"I'm going out with Chelsea and Ryan to a party," I said.

"Sounds like fun, and I know you will be careful," he said.

"Always, Dad," I replied with a smile. I didn't want him to worry about me, especially because of what my mother puts him through.

When we got back home, I ran upstairs to figure out what I was going to wear to this shindig. I wanted something flirty but not slutty. I ended up with my skinny jeans, a white tank top, my black blazer, and my red pumps. I figured if I fall at the party, people will just think I'm drunk. I threw on some jewelry and before I could even put on my makeup, Ryan and his brother were honking in my driveway. I threw some lip gloss in my purse to put on later.

"Hey guys," I said as I got into the car. Ryan's brother James just smiled and I could barely hear his voice when he said hello. He was soft-spoken and shy, nothing like Ryan.

"Why do you girls feel the need to always wear makeup?" Ryan asked as I glided my lip gloss across my lips.

"Well, this lip gloss is a necessity."

"And why is that?" asked Ryan. "It tastes like Passion Mango," I said flirtatiously.

"You are planning on licking your lips all night?" he questioned. "No, but I do plan on kissing some very hot stranger," I said.

Ryan laughed and said, "You do realize there will be no guys that interest you at this party."

"What's that supposed to mean?" I asked sarcastically.

"They are all drunken frat boys who just want to stand on their heads and drink out of a keg all night thinking that's cool. They are totally not your type," he explained as if he knew my type.

"I think I want to stand on my head tonight and drink out of a keg," I said with a laugh.

"Where is Anna? I think we may have picked up the wrong girl!" Ryan was teasing. I punched him softly in the arm as we went to go pick up Chelsea.

Ryan was right. All the guys at this party were immature, drunken college boys. Chelsea, of course, mingled right in. My plan of kissing anyone went right out the door as soon as I walked in the place. Perhaps I needed an older gent. I still tried to have fun though. Sometimes I hated that I was more mature. Chelsea made her drunken way over to me and asked why I was not "getting it on" with one of the gorgeous guys at the party. I told her that I was still figuring out which one I wanted to take home. She was getting pretty cozy with one guy who reminded me of a younger Tom Cruise. He was cute and definitely more her style.

"So how's the flavored lipstick working out for you?" Ryan asked with funny sarcasm.

"It tastes pretty good. I've been licking my own lips all night," I said.

"I told you. These guys are no good for you, Anna."

"What about you? No drunken girls catching your attention?"

"Nah, I thought one girl was pretty close but then she started kissing her friend," he said.

"Oh, she already had a man?"

"Nope, another girl," he explained.

"I thought you guys were into that kind of kinky pleasure..."

"Most guys are and it's fun to watch but like you, Anna, I'm looking for more than just this," he said as he pointed around the room.

Ryan was one of the good ones for sure. It's too bad we were so close because he would be the perfect guy. I would never want to jeopardize our friendship. I felt that some friendships were more meaningful than romantic relationships. I looked over at his brother James, who just stood in the corner and people-watched.

"What's up with James?" I asked. "You think he will ever find a girlfriend?"

"I don't know. He's too shy to talk to girls for some reason and I know for a fact he isn't gay. I kind of feel bad for him," Ryan explained.

"Like Chelsea says, there is someone out there for everyone."

"I guess so," Ryan replied. "Speaking of Chelsea, should we go and break up her romantic one-nighter man?"

"Yeah, I'm pretty tired." I really was.

* * *

When I got back home, my father was lying on the couch watching television just as I expected. I walked over to him and kissed his forehead. "Goodnight Daddy."

He sat up and asked, "Did you have a good time at the party?"

"It was fine, just your normal college frat party," I said.

"I'm glad you're home safe. Goodnight Anna Banana," he said as he hugged me.

I haven't heard him call me Anna Banana in a long time. It must have been an emotional day for him too. He probably realizes that soon I will be leaving the house and starting my own life. I felt bad for him and where he was in his own relationship. He should be enjoying this time and looking forward to retirement. Instead, his wife is in rehab and he is mourning the loss of his mother.

The only thing my dad enjoys is his workshop out in the garage.

He loves creating things out of wood. His great-grandfather was a skilled carpenter and made beautiful rocking chairs. My father inherited all of his woodworking tools and since then it's been his hobby. He made my mom a mahogany jewelry box last Christmas. He carved out a heart made in cherry and glued it to the top. For my seventh birthday he presented me with a handmade dollhouse. Grandma actually sewed all the decorations for the inside, like the little sofas and bedding. I cherish that dollhouse.

As I laid in bed, I could not sleep. I stared up at my ceiling at those cheap plastic stars again. Then I remembered that unopened envelope that was addressed to my grandmother. I sat up and turned on the lamp. I reached over for my laptop bag and pulled out the envelope. I glanced at it for a minute, wondering if it was wrong to open it. Then I thought there must be a reason I found it. I slowly ripped it open and pulled out a written letter. It was in very neat cursive writing and addressed to Jeanie Corolla. It read:

Dear Jeanie,

I am not sure where to begin. This is your cousin, Freda Mills, in Dunkirk, Indiana. My mother, your Aunt Flora, recently passed away at the ripe age of 101. My mother became interested in genealogy the last few years of her life and discovered information I really need to share with you. One fact she learned about will change your life in the most positive way. I could not find a telephone number listed for you so I am hoping I have your correct home address. If you can call me here in Indiana when you receive this letter, it's very important that I converse with you. I will look forward to your call. God Bless.

Love your cousin,

Freda Mills

002-555-3397

My mind was running on overdrive. What could this lady possibly have wanted to share with my grandmother? She said it was important. I wondered if I should call her but then my family might be upset that I went ahead and stole a letter that was meant for my grandmother's eyes. I just sat there and looked at the letter as the words sort of bunched together and became blurry.

What have I done? I can't put the letter back and just forget about it. Was there a reason that I opened it? Was my grandmother sending me some sort of sign from Heaven to find this important information?

I put the letter back in the envelope and into the top drawer of my nightstand. I shut off my lamp and pulled the covers over me. I felt chills all over my body. My eyes were heavy but I had a hard time falling asleep that night.

CHAPTER SEVEN

"Sleep well?" my father asked as I reached for a mug out of the cabinet. I poured some coffee and sat down at the table. "No, not really Dad," I answered. He looked up at me puzzled and asked, "Why not?" I shrugged my shoulders, "I don't know. A lot on my mind, I guess."

"I understand," he said as he got up from the table and put on his sports jacket. "I have to run into work for a meeting and then I'm driving up to the rehab center."

"I thought they didn't allow visitors?" I asked, confused.

"They don't. I'm going there to meet with her case worker. She will let me know how she's doing and if we need to extend her treatment."

My dad looked really stressed out. "You okay Dad?" I asked.

"Don't you worry about me, Anna. I'm a grown man and these are just hurdles in life. Everyone has problems but how we handle them says a lot about our character."

I walked over to my dad and gave him a hug. "Dad, you have great character," I said. He gave me a tight squeeze and walked out the door.

I went into the living room and plopped myself onto the couch. I decided to turn on the TV since I barely ever had time to watch it. As I flipped through the channels, I realized why I never watched since it was all junk. I stared at it for awhile but then my mind wandered again about that letter. A commercial came on for a company out in Indiana. *Hmm, that's funny. That is exactly where the letter came from, a cousin in Indiana. Was this a sign? Why would a TV station in Connecticut be advertising for a company out in Indiana?* It was driving me crazy and I had to tell someone about this letter. Just then the phone rang.

"Hello?" my voice cracked a little.

"Anna?" I recognized the voice immediately. It was my Aunt Sharon. She sounded a bit stressed. "Hey, how are you?" I asked.

"Terrible. Is your father home?"

"No, he just left for some meeting and then was going to drive to the rehab center," I explained. "Everything okay?" There was a pause for a moment and then tears. I always know when people cry over the phone. "What's going on?" I asked again.

I could hear her sniff in her runny nose as she began to explain why she was upset. It had to do with my Aunt Vivian again and reading my grandmother's will.

"Her family is all about the goddamn money. She can have the freaking money, Anna. I don't want a dime of it. I just want my mother back," she said with a burst of tears.

One of the problems with getting older is that you realize how many issues your family really does have. As a child, you only see or pay attention to the good stuff. You don't understand any of the drama. If only we could turn back time and enjoy our childhood for a little while longer. I felt bad for Aunt Sharon as she vented to me about our family.

"What does Poppy want to do?" I asked.

"He doesn't know, Anna. He is so brainwashed from my damn sister that he will go along with anything she says."

This was probably true. My grandfather was reliant on others to make decisions for him because my grandmother took care of everything.

"I think out of respect for Poppy, Grandma's will shouldn't be seen as the priority right now," I explained.

"Exactly, Anna, but try telling that to your Aunt Vivian. She just has dollar signs flashing in her pupils. She's been talking about buying a retirement home down in South Carolina. She probably wants the money for that reason," Aunt Sharon explained.

"Grandma deserves more than that," I said. I wondered why my Aunt Vivian was acting so cold. I tried hard to reason with people, considering I'd be studying them for a living. She wasn't completely heartless but I couldn't understand why she had to read the will now. Aunt Vivian has a good job and has her own money. I can't see her needing the money for a retirement home, and she's only fifty-six.

"Maybe her way of dealing with the loss is being all about the business side and getting everything over with," I said to Aunt Sharon.

"No, Anna, she is just a bitch. Always has been and always will be. I can't even stand to look at her right now," she replied.

It's sad to think that when people die, family members start looking for handouts. Our conversation made me upset, especially because we just had a nice lunch after my graduation. I guess some people are good at acting when they need to. After I hung up the phone, I sat on the couch and cried.

What a mess. I pulled out an old family album and started looking through the pictures. They were from Christmas of 1999. We always celebrated Christmas at my grandparents' house. My grandmother made the best lasagna and her chocolate mayonnaise cake melted in your mouth. As I looked through the pictures, everyone seemed so happy. There was laughter and hugs and pictures that portrayed the family we once were. As I closed the album I knew that it could never be like that again. When you lose the glue that holds a family together, it's not easy to fix it, especially when that person is irreplaceable.

That night I had the strangest dream. My grandmother came to visit me. It was one of those dreams where you feel like a message was given to you but you can't quite seem to put the pieces together. I remembered sitting outside with my grandmother on the bench. I told her how much I missed her and that everything in the family was falling apart. She told me it would all work out and that I would find a hidden treasure. What was that supposed to mean? Maybe it pertained to all the money that everyone was trying to get their hands on. I studied dreams in one of my college courses. What I learned was that there was no solid answer about why we dream about certain things. Sometimes we dream in fear or love and sometimes we don't dream at all. I knew I had to stop thinking so hard, and I was running late for my meeting with Chelsea at Starbucks. I threw on some jeans and an oversized college sweatshirt and out the door I went.

* * *

There was Chelsea, already sipping her mocha-latte and engrossed in her iPad. She took that thing everywhere she went.

"Sorry I'm late, Chels," I said as I took a seat across from her.

"You are not going to get anything?" she asked.

"Nah, not right now."

"They just took out a batch of those chocolate chip muffins you like," she said.

That was Chelsea, always trying to talk me into something. She'd be a great salesperson.

"I'm not that hungry," I replied. Chelsea knew right away something was bothering me. She looked up from her iPad and said, "Okay, spill the beans, what is going on with you today?" I took a deep breath and said, "Nothing really."

"Anna, it's me you're talking to. I know everything there is to know about you and something is up, so what's the deal?"

"I had a weird dream last night. My grandmother came to visit me."

"That's great, Anna. I read somewhere that people who had passed on will sometimes visit their loved ones in their dreams. What did she say?"

"I don't know. It's hard to remember but we were sitting on a bench and I was telling her about how messed up the family has been. Then she said that I will find a hidden treasure to make it better."

"A hidden treasure, eh? What do you think that means?" Chelsea asked.

"Well, I never told you this, but when I was over my Poppy's house printing out my thesis, I found a letter. It was for my grandmother but had never been opened," I explained.

"Did you open it?" Chelsea asked curiously.

"I did."

"And what was it about?"

"It was from a cousin out in Indiana who said she needed to speak with her right away about some news she had."

"Did you tell anyone about the letter?" she asked.

"No, and I sort of feel bad about it. The family has just been insane lately with arguments and hostility. It's like I don't even recognize them anymore," I sadly explained.

"It will get better. People are mourning and it's a huge loss. What else did the letter say? Did it give you any clues?" Chelsea questioned as she sipped her latte.

"She did mention that she came across the news because her mother was into genealogy."

"So it has something to do with your family history," Chelsea said. It seemed like her mind wandered off for a minute and then she blurted out, "Sounds crazy but maybe the hidden treasure has something to do with that letter. You have to go there and see what it is."

"What am I supposed to do, just take off to Indiana and find this cousin I don't even know?" I asked.

"Yeah, what do you have to lose?" she replied.

"What if this person is a psychopath or tells me something horrible?" I asked.

"What if she tells you something amazing or special about your grandmother? There was a reason you found that letter, Anna, and now your grandmother basically told you in a dream to go find out what it's all about."

Leave it to Chelsea to bring on the drama or movie-like setting. I decided to go up to the counter and get one of those chocolate chip muffins. I sat there eating my muffin and drinking chamomile tea. I didn't like tea very much but figured it may calm me down. I thought to myself, *Could I really drive all the way to Indiana by myself and look for this person? What if it really would make a difference to my family, could it possibly fix what's been broken?*

On my way home from meeting with Chelsea, I decided to visit my Poppy. I brought him a pepper and egg sub. It was his favorite and it made him happy. He told me about a new Italian music group he saw on television last night that he really liked. It was nice having a normal conversation with someone for once. He tried teaching me some Italian words and talked about his mother and father who were born and raised in Sicilia. It was nice listening to him talk about his parents. It made me think about the letter, though. I tried to forget about it and just enjoy the visit. Just then, the door swung open and Aunt Sharon walked in. She looked disgusted. I knew that would be the end of our nice conversation.

"Hi Auntie Sharon," I said. She sat down at the table with us and asked Poppy about the will.

"Dad, will you please tell me the truth about whether or not you are prepared and ready to deal with Ma's will?" Poppy looked down in his lap and seemed confused. "Dad, it's okay if you don't want to deal with it now but you have to tell Vivian. She has become overly obsessed with all of this and you know it," she said.

"What do you want me to say?" Poppy replied. He looked so sad. "I want you to be honest with me and stop letting others make up your mind," she explained.

"Well Vivian is the Executor of the estate so whatever she wants to do is fine," Poppy said as he threw up his hands.

"Dad, just because she is the Executor, that does not give her the right to rule over you. You are not dead!" yelled Auntie Sharon. My grandfather shrugged his shoulders and said, "Not yet, but who knows how long I will be here."

All this talk was paining my heart. I walked into the living room and looked at a picture of my grandmother on the wall. She looked so happy. It was strange being in that house without her. I found myself talking to her picture. "What am I supposed to do now, Grandma?"

As I heard the bickering between my grandfather and my aunt, I just wanted to run away. My father was in Vermont with my mother because of issues and even here I couldn't escape the bullshit. I turned around and saw a decorative plate sitting on the end table. There were words on it: *Indiana, the Crossroads of America*. At that moment, I knew what I had to do. I was going to leave this place—leave the drama, the tears, the bickering, and set out to Indiana.

I left my grandfather's house and headed over to Ryan's. I wanted him to look over my car to make sure it would even make the eight hundred miles.

"You are going where?" he asked me. "I'm going to drive to Indiana to visit a cousin," I explained.

"Of all the places you can travel, you pick farmland? Sounds like a fun trip," he said with a smirk.

"Hey, there is something I need to do there that has to do with my grandmother. It's where she grew up and her parents are buried there so I want to visit," I said.

"Whatever floats your boat, Anna. It's a long drive to see cows and cornfields but looks like old Betty will make the drive," he said as he closed my hood. I gave him a big hug and thanked him a gazillion times. "You need to be careful, though, and make sure you have Triple A, or some backup if you happen to stall."

"Don't worry. If I stall, I am sure some good-hearted Midwestern boy will come to my rescue," I said teasingly.

"Like the hot frat guy you were hoping to share your flavored lip gloss with. Bring pepper spray and a baseball bat," he joked.

"You are too much, Ry. I will be fine and I appreciate your concerns. I can do this. I really need to get out of here for awhile" I explained.

"Just be safe and call if you need anything," he said as he squeezed me tight.

I left Ryan's and went home to pack a bag. I wasn't sure how long I would be gone so I packed for what seemed like a month. I opened my bottom desk drawer to find my emergency stash of cash. It was another tip I learned from my grandmother. She always kept money hidden all over the house in case of an emergency or just for a rainy day. There was about seven hundred dollars in that envelope so I figured it would be good for gas and food. I was recently approved for my first credit card so I could charge a hotel stay if need be. My parents never used credit cards but how would I ever get any credit if I didn't use one? Besides, I would just pay it right off anyway when I got back home.

I went into the kitchen and packed a small cooler with bottled water and snacks in case I got hungry. My father still wasn't home and I was glad. I really didn't want to have to talk him into letting me go. I had to leave him a note, but what would I say. "Hey, I found a letter and I'm going to search for the hidden message?" I did what any girl would do to protect her father from worrying. I lied and told him I was taking a little road trip to clear my head. I explained that between Grandma's passing and Mom in rehab, I just needed a break. A deep feeling of guilt came over me as I sealed the letter into the envelope.

Would he be angry with me or would this stress him out even more? He was also dealing with issues and here I was taking off on him. A teardrop fell from my eyes and onto the shiny wood finish upon our kitchen table. My mind kept telling me to unpack and stay but my heart told me to go. Which one do I follow? Both options have valid reasons so I guess this is what choosing your path in life means. If I stay, it would be easier and less dangerous but I may never know what information is crucial to our family. If I go, I get to meet a new relative and learn more about my grandmother's family. I wiped the tears from my eyes, took a deep breath, grabbed my bags, and was on my way.

I threw my duffel bag into the trunk and kept the cooler with me. It was dark and the thought of driving in places I have never been before in the dark was making me anxious. As I turned the key, I told myself, *Come on Anna; Put your "big girl panties" on.* I pulled out of my driveway and turned on the radio. I started blurting out the words of the song that was playing to help relieve my nervousness. "Hey baby, there ain't no easy way out." It was probably a sign from God that this trip was not going to be easy.

CHAPTER EIGHT

I had been driving almost four hours already. The roads were empty except for the truckers. I thought about the job of a trucker. It must be nice being on the open road, no boss hovering over you, seeing so much of the country. Then I thought about driving in snowstorms or horrid traffic. I would not want to deal with that.

As I pulled up alongside a truck with a picture of potato chips on the side, suddenly I was hungry. I reached over and unzipped the cooler. I pulled out some veggie sticks. *Crunch, crunch, crunch,* boy were they good. I knew that even though the makers of the veggie chip dynasty marketed these chips as being "healthy," they certainly were not. Of course, they were better than regular potato chips—then again, I'm sure I ate twice the serving size.

I opened up a bottle of water and took a drink. I tried not to drink a lot while I was traveling because I hated having to stop and pee. At times you can get stuck at those gas stations where you wonder if the toilets have ever been cleaned because the whole room smells like urine. Thinking about that ruined my appetite so I put the bag of chips away.

I let out a loud yawn and rubbed my eyes. I was getting tired. The GPS was telling me I had another two hundred and twenty miles on the I-80 highway. I didn't want to fall asleep at the wheel so I started looking for hotels. Luckily, another two miles ahead there was a little town called Danville. I found a place that looked decent so I pulled in. I parked right in front since walking into hotels in the middle of the night was creepy. When I opened the doors, it was very quiet and I wondered if anyone was around. Then this younger woman appeared from the back and said in the cutest accent, "Welcome, are you checking in?"

"I am hoping you have a vacancy?" I asked with an exhausted smile.

"We sure do, darling. Let me see what I can get for you."

I stood there half asleep as she was smiling ear to ear. I wondered how her time clock was functioning this peppy at almost three o'clock in the morning.

"Do you have any company or are you alone?" she asked. "Just me," I replied.

"Okay, I have a standard room, with a king-size bed, free wifi, and a fridge for $89, plus tax." At this point I just wanted to see a bed to sleep in. "That would be perfect," I answered.

"Great, here is the key and it's Room 101, which is right around the corner here."

I have to say I was glad to be near the lobby. I never stayed in a hotel by myself before.

"We also offer free coffee in the lobby every morning starting at 5:00 a.m.," she said again with such spunk. I swore she was on something.

"I may need that in the morning. Thanks again for your help," I replied as I took my bag and made my way to Room 101.

I opened the door after it took me about five times swiping the stupid hotel key card. It's always a gamble to determine if you have swiped the card the right way so that the little green light goes on. Then you have to rush to open the door so you don't get stuck swiping again. As I turned on the lights, I was never happier to see a bed. I quickly washed my face and brushed my teeth. I took off my bootleg Uggs and I laid down. My eyes were slowly starting to close but then I wondered what my father thought about me running off and just leaving him a note. It felt like a cop out. In the world of technology that we live in, one would think I could simply have called him. Then I wondered why he hadn't tried calling me. Was he furious? Had he even found my note? I thought about all kinds of god-awful things. It was too late to call him now so I figured maybe a text would be alright. I wanted him to know I was okay. I hit Send and then plugged my phone into the charger and set my alarm for 7:00 a.m. It wouldn't give me a good night's rest but I didn't want to get on the road too late. I turned out the lights and fell right to sleep.

It felt as if I had been asleep for only ten minutes before my annoying alarm went off. I really hated that sound but it seemed to always get me out of bed, probably because it made a sound like a fire alarm and after hearing something that annoying in the morning, who could then rustle back to sleep? I could hear the sound of the showers running in other rooms above me. I checked my phone to see if I had any messages from Dad. Sure enough, one had come through at 5:15 in the morning.

My dad always woke up early. The man could survive on only four hours of sleep. I wish I had that same luck. I opened up the text and he said that he received my note and though he was not particularly happy with my decision, he knows I'm an adult. He asked that I be careful and to please call him as soon as I could. Some kids think their parents are annoying with all the phone calls and the "checking in" but I liked that my dad was protective. As I got older I seemed to have more appreciation for my parents than I did at eighteen. It was probably because I finally understood that they were right and I should have listened to them more.

I cranked on the shower and waited for it to get hot. I grabbed my little bottle of soap and my loofah and washed away. I could stand in the shower for hours. It was soothing letting the water spray down on my skin. I thought about the long drive ahead and wondered why on earth I didn't think to take Chelsea with me. She was my best friend and would have kept me company. I had never been on my own like this before. I suddenly began to feel a little lonely. I rinsed the soap off my face and turned the water off. I threw on a pair of my favorite ripped jeans and a T-shirt. I put on my hoodie in case it was chilly and packed up my things.

In the hotel lobby I found the coffee station and boy, was I glad to see that. They had all kinds of flavors, from Irish Cream to Hazelnut, French Vanilla, and even Mocha. I went with the French Vanilla because chocolate in the morning just doesn't seem right. Much to my surprise, that same girl who was at the front desk last night was still there. She was even wearing that hyper sort of smile too as the guests passed by her. I wondered what she was like when she got home. Did she just crash on her couch? Or maybe she went home to a husband and kids, or to her parents? Then again, she could have lived alone. We pass by lots of different people every day, yet we never really get to know who they are. Even though I was surrounded by strangers in this lobby, it was nice not to be alone.

When I got into my car and turned the key, I couldn't help but think about my grandma again. She enjoyed traveling but never got to do it much because my Poppy was a homebody. I strapped on my seatbelt and fired up the engine. I plugged in my iPod and the tunes started playing. I loved having an iPod—it was so much easier than changing CD's. I still remember when I would record music right from the radio onto a cassette. Those days were long gone.

I drove onto the ramp that brought me right back to Highway I-80. It felt like I was driving on a treadmill, going nowhere fast. I tried my best to enjoy the ride and the scenery. Some of the mountains were pretty astonishing to look at. I thought about all the people who drive on this road and probably miss all the beauty because life is a constant rush. I made a vow to myself at that moment to slow down every now and then because I may miss out on something breathtaking. As I was feeling all philosophical, my cell phone rang. It was my Aunt Sharon. I didn't want to answer it at first because I hated lying to my family. She probably wondered what on earth I was thinking just leaving town like I did. I answered the call.

As I suspected, she questioned where I was. I told her I was near Cleveland, Ohio, and was thinking of checking out the Rock and Roll Hall of Fame. To my surprise, she said she wished she had come with me. She wanted to run away and leave behind all the drama. I felt guilty in a way, skipping out of town, knowing all the stress she had too. We both have always been there for each other like best friends.

I listened for awhile as she went on about how Aunt Vivian went to see the lawyer again and she just wished all the chaos would go away. Then she spoke of my grandmother and how much she missed her through all this. It was hard not to tear up but I had to focus on driving. I was already feeling a bit like a criminal talking on my cell phone. I didn't have one of those earpieces. All of a sudden, my phone died. "Hello, *Hello?*"

Oh my word, what just happened? I pulled the phone away from my ear and saw that it had turned off. I pressed the On button but nothing was working. This was not good. I kept trying to fix it but I still had to focus on the road. I put the phone down and started to panic. *What if Auntie Sharon thinks I was in an accident?* I'm sure she has tried calling me back. I had to find a rest stop or a gas station to make a call and fiddle with this stupid phone. It seemed like every exit was about ten miles apart. This was just my luck.

Finally, I saw a sign for food and gas so I pulled off the exit. There was a gas station right there so I drove in. Luckily, they had a pay phone. Even pay phones were hard to come by. Now I had to scavenge around my car to find enough change to make a toll call. I felt like it was 1995 in the days of beepers and huge cell phones that only rich people could afford. I walked up to the pay phone and put in my change. *Please pick up,* I thought as I heard the phone ringing.

"Anna, is that you?" Auntie Sharon asked. "Yes, it's me."

"Where in God's name are you? This isn't your cell phone number, what happened?"

"My phone just went dead and I can't turn it back on. I'm not sure what's wrong with it. I don't want you or my father to worry so please let him know too that I'm okay."

"What are you going to do, Anna, without a cell phone, driving around the country all by yourself? It's simply not safe." Auntie Sharon had a great point.

"I know. I'll think of something. Once I get closer to Cleveland, I'm sure they will have cell phone stores so I'll just pick up a replacement phone for now."

Just then, that stupid recording came on, saying I had only one minute left unless I put in more coins. "Auntie Sharon, I am all out of change and I literally have one more minute before we disconnect."

"Anna. Just make sure you get a new phone as soon as you can and I'll let your dad know."

"Thanks so much. Tell everyone I love them," I said.

"I will. And Anna, please, please, please be careful," she asked with worry in her voice.

"I promise," I replied as the call ended.

* * *

I walked into the convenience store because I had this sudden craving for a Ring Ding. They were so good. I grabbed a bottle of water and my sinful snack and walked up to the register. The girl behind the counter was a bit odd. She looked like she belonged to some sort of mean girl street gang. I don't even think she looked up at me when I said "good afternoon." I wondered what she was thinking. Maybe she hated her job, her parents, her life, or maybe it was all a tough-girl act. I wouldn't feel comfortable working at a gas station. They get robbed all the time. The brother of one of my friends worked at one and was held up at gunpoint. I started to feel bad for her as I took my change, and I smiled as I walked out.

I opened my car door and got inside. I sat for a minute and opened my Ring Dings before starting the car. I took a bit of that chocolate covered cake and I was in Heaven, though it would have tasted much better with milk. When I was a kid I would always dunk my Ring Dings into milk. I loved junk food. Something about it just made me happy. They say sugar is like a poison and it's addictive. I took a sip of my water and decided to hit the road.

Not long after I got back onto the highway, I ran into heavy traffic. I saw an alert sign pop up that there was construction two miles ahead. They always seem to work on the roads at the most inconvenient times. I get it, they have to do their jobs too, but somehow I was always the person who got stuck in traffic. I can understand major road rage, especially when there are accidents and everyone feels the need to stop and take a look before moving on.

I looked at the people in the cars slowly driving by next to me. I wondered what their lives were like, where they were headed, if their day was stressful or full of happiness. The truth is we are all just trying to live our lives. I noticed a little girl in the car next to me. She was looking out the window with such a big smile on her face. It made me miss being a kid. She looked as if she had not a single worry in this world. I wanted to roll down my window and tell her to enjoy those moments. Soon enough, she will be me—graduated and clueless.

I drove on for another few hours before growing tired again. I was hoping to get a good night's rest since I was already more than halfway to Indiana. I also had to remember that I had a broken phone so I didn't want to take any chances. A couple of exits up, I found a few options to rest my eyes. One hotel looked to have a good restaurant attached to it so I decided to stay there. Finally, I found a place with a normal-looking person behind the counter. He had been reading what looked to be a college book. Maybe he was working there nights while finishing up his degree.

"Can I help you, Miss?" He had a warm smile and a kind voice. It definitely made me feel better about checking into this hotel.

"I would like a room for tonight please, non-smoking," I replied.

"I'm sure I can help you with that," he said. "I have a queen-size bed, non-smoking, on the third floor. I can give you the discount rate of $79, plus tax," he explained.

"Thank you so much, that will be just fine," I said as I handed him my credit card.

"What time does the restaurant close?" I asked. "The kitchen stays open till 11:00," he said as he handed me back my card. I took my room key and headed up to the third floor.

I decided to go to the restaurant and have a bite to eat. I wanted something different besides fast-food. I ordered a chicken dish with veggies on the side. I had to make sure I was getting proper nutrition and not just Ring Dings.

The restaurant was nice and quiet. Only a few people were in there dining—mostly people like me, all alone. They had the TV's on so I started watching Family Feud. I loved that show. Soon enough, my food came and it looked wonderful. It was nice sitting there enjoying a meal but I still felt lonely. The other people had reading materials or were on their phones. That reminded me that I should call my father, first thing in the morning.

CHAPTER NINE

I made my way down to the front desk to check out and I asked the clerk where the closest cell phone store was. The man laughed and said, "Sweetie, you are far from home, aren't 'cha?"

I had no idea what he meant by that. Every cell phone commercial you see claims to have service all over the U.S. He told me the closest mall was two hours away and they should have what I was looking for. I couldn't believe it. Two hours away! How do these people live? I asked him if there was a pay phone around that I could use. He told me there were some around the corner near the bathrooms, so I walked over to call my dad.

"Hello?" My father answered cautiously. I could only imagine what he was thinking when this phone number showed up on the caller ID. "Hi Dad, it's Anna."

"Anna." He sounded relieved. "I'm so glad you called. Sharon told me about your cell phone. Is this your new number or something?"

"Sadly, no Dad, I am using the hotel pay phone. The clerk told me the closest cell phone store is about two hours away," I explained.

"*Two hours!*" he yelled. "Where in the world are you, Anna?"

"Dad, I'm in Ohio, but in the country. Don't worry, everything is okay," I said as I tried calming him down. I hated worrying my father.

He took a deep breath and said, "Okay, I can't help but worry. It would have been easier if you took someone with you, like Chelsea. I don't feel safe with you on the road all alone but I do understand why you left. Please just call me every day and get yourself a cell phone as soon as you can. How are you with money?" he asked.

"I'm all set Dad, and thanks for worrying. I'll be home soon," I said as I hung up the phone. After that call I just wanted to get this trip over and done with. The guilt was hard to handle.

I got into my car and wished there was a Dunkin' Donuts around this place. The hotel lobby coffee wasn't cutting it for me. I figured that any chance of a decent coffee place around here was slim to none. I opened my lukewarm cooler and pulled out a bottle of water.

I passed farm after farm and everything was flat. I saw a huge trailer truck with three trailers attached. I would never want to drive one of those things. How do people even maneuver them? I was glad it wasn't dark out. There were a lot of trucks driving around me and I get anxious, especially in the dark. I started to get hungry. That was the problem with long road trips. The driving gets boring quickly, and eating breaks up the monotony. There had to be something to eat with all these farms around. I saw a sign for a little diner two exits up.

I pulled off the exit for the diner and turned into this little hole-in-the-wall place. At this point, I didn't care what they served as long as they had coffee. When I walked in, there was a little breakfast bar and some tables set up. It looked okay to me. The waitress asked me if I wanted to sit but I had no time to waste so I ordered a coffee and an egg and cheese sandwich to go. I browsed around while waiting. They had a rack of postcards, which I thought was strange. I mean, who visits this place long enough to want a postcard? I saw one, though, that I had to buy. It said, "Life's a Cow so Stop your Mooing." I felt I could share that one with lots of people, mostly my own family.

"Okay dear, here is your coffee and sandwich. Can I get you anything else?" she asked. "Just this postcard please," I said as I handed it over to her.

"This is a good one. We have a lot of moo'ers who come in here." she laughed.

"I think we all know a lot of people who do too much of that," I replied back. She was a real nice lady. Maybe these old hick towns weren't so bad. She handed me my things and I handed her a ten. "Keep the change," I said as I walked out. Even though my stuff only came to $5.85, I felt the need to leave a tip. Pay it forward.

I sat in my car and ate that sandwich like I hadn't eaten in days. The coffee was still a bit too hot but I sipped it anyway and burnt the bejesus out of my tongue. I watched the people going in and out of this place. Some looked completely normal and others I questioned. I've always been a city girl but there was something peaceful about this area. I'm not sure I could live here, but I felt relaxed.

I pulled back onto the highway and started to hear a knocking sound. I thought, *what the heck is that?* I tried to ignore it as I stepped on the gas to get moving. Maybe it was just from all the sand in that driveway that kicked up into my motor. I looked at my clock and it was already noontime. I had another hour to drive before I even reached the mall area. It seemed like it was taking forever to drive through these big states. From New England, you can get just about anywhere in an hour. I guess that makes us a bit spoiled.

Up ahead I saw signs that said "One Lane" and "Detour." This was just great. Traffic slowed down and started piling up. I checked my gas tank and sure enough, I was running low. I didn't want to chance it in this traffic because I wasn't sure how long I'd be stuck in it. I had to get off an exit and hope a gas station was nearby. Usually, my GPS could find gas stations but the smaller mom-and-pop shops weren't coming up.

There was an exit a mile up the road and I decided to take a chance. As I got off the ramp, I realized it probably wasn't the best one to take. I began to drive up the road, hoping to find some signs of life. I heard that knocking noise again so I decided to pull to the side of the road and open the hood. I wanted to see if there was sand in there or something that didn't look right. I knew a little bit about cars, like how to check my oil but that was about it.

As I popped the hood, I looked around the engine and other parts to see if anything was different. I didn't notice any sand but I cleared out a few dead leaves, and hoped maybe that was the problem. I got back into the car and turned the key. "Uh, oh! Come on baby, start, please," I begged of the car.

After a few unsuccessful tries, I realized the engine was completely dead. Maybe it was the battery or worse, the starter. Either way, I was officially stranded. The worst part was that it was in a place I had never been before that was as lifeless as the leaves I pulled out from my hood. I went back outside and again looked under the hood of the car. My heart began to race and I felt my body weaken. I wanted my Daddy. As if things couldn't get any worse, I felt a drop on my arm.

"Anything else you want to throw my way?" I yelled up at the sky as I started to cry. I couldn't hold back the tears. They poured out of me just as fast as the rain was falling from the sky. I had no phone, no car, and I was all alone. Maybe that dream wasn't really a sign. I should have just stayed home and told my family about the stupid letter.

Suddenly, my racing heart went into overdrive. A pickup truck pulled over to the side of the road and a man had stepped out. I could tell it was a man by his physique and the boots he was wearing. I couldn't see much of anything else through the rainy fog and my tears. I tried to compose myself and stand up while wiping my eyes dry but the raindrops didn't help matters. My adrenaline was flowing. I had no pepper spray, no baseball bat, just the one gym class that taught me simple self-defense tricks. How I wished I was home curled up in my bed. I prayed that this person was not some sort of psycho killer.

As he stepped in closer, I got a glimpse of his face. He had dirty blonde hair that was covered up with a trucker's hat curled up around the rim. His boyish face made him look merely seventeen. It took some of the worry away. He smiled at me and then spoke in this adorable country boy accent, "Miss, are you having car trouble?"

Feeling quite embarrassed and probably looking like a hot mess, I simply replied, "Yes, yes I am."

He sort of laughed and asked, "What are you doing standing out here in the pouring rain?"

"I was trying to fix my car but realized it wasn't going to happen," I answered with a slight touch of laughter. I think he could tell I was anxious so he did his best to make me more comfortable.

"My name is Brady and I live here in town. My dad owns an auto body shop a few miles down the road. Since it's raining, do you mind if we get in my truck so we can discuss your car problem? I don't want you catching a cold out here in the rain, and I promise that I'm a total gentleman," he said as he flashed that boyish smile.

I thought to myself, *What other choice do I have at this moment, and he seems okay.* Then he reached into his pocket and showed me his driver's license and his business card. "I'm an honest guy, really," he said.

"Thanks for showing me that. It's just, I don't know where I am, and I guess I watch too many shows with serial killers," I said with a slight chuckle.

He laughed and said, "I understand. I watch those shows too and I would be a little scared as well. If it makes you feel better, I can just go get the tow truck while you wait with your car. I just didn't want to leave you out here in the rain all alone," he explained.

"No it's fine, I'll go with you. I appreciate your understanding," I said. He walked over to the passenger side of his truck and opened the car door for me. He was a gentleman. Men opening car doors for ladies is as common as having to physically walk over to change the television channel versus using a remote. As he got into his truck he handed me a paper towel to dry my face. "I'm sorry, it's all I have to help you dry off."

"It's okay, I appreciate the paper towel. I'm Anna, by the way. Thanks for stopping to help me," I said with a shy smile.

"You're welcome. So what happened with your car?" he asked.

"I'm not sure. It started making this knocking sound. At first I ignored it but when I saw the highway was backed up with traffic I didn't want to get stuck so I pulled off this exit," I explained.

Brady laughed with this amazing smile and said, "Yeah, this part of town doesn't get too much traffic. Does the car start at all?" he asked.

"No, after I checked under the hood and removed some dead leaves, I got back inside and it wouldn't even turn over," I replied.

"Hmm, well, normally, one would think it is the battery but since it also had a knocking sound, I doubt that's the problem. The leaves probably didn't cause the knocking sound but good thinking to remove them," Brady said.

"Thanks, I'm not much of a car connoisseur," I replied.

"It's okay, most women aren't, and I must say, a lot of guys are not either," he laughed.

"Thanks I feel better," I said.

"We can have your car towed to my dad's shop to take a look, if you are okay with that?" Brady asked.

"Sounds good to me, thanks for your help," I said. I was surprised at how easy it was to strike up a conversation with him. He told me a little about his family and his dad's business. We talked about how long he has lived in Ohio and that he hasn't traveled much.

"If you don't mind me asking, where were you going? I noticed your license plate wasn't from Ohio," he said.

"I am on my way to Portland, Indiana, to see a relative of mine," I replied.

"I bet you're wishing you flew there now instead of driving," he said.

"Yeah, that definitely would have been the better option. But this trip was a spur of the moment thing so I just jumped in my car and left," I answered.

Brady looked puzzled at my response. "You just jumped in your car and took off?

"It's kind of a long story, but I'm on my way to meet a relative that I've never met before."

"So if you don't mind me asking, what makes you want to meet this relative?" he asked.

"My grandmother recently passed away and she lived in Indiana till she was nine years old. She always wanted to go back and visit. I wanted to take this trip with her but when she got sick, it wasn't feasible," I explained.

"So you're doing this trip for her, sort of like a closure?" Brady suggested.

"Yeah, I guess you can say that. There is a little more to my story but we'd need a few hours," I laughed.

"Well, if you end up spending some time here in Ohio, maybe you can share your story with me."

Wow, a boy who actually wants to listen to a girl talk. Where did this guy come from? It started to feel like a fairy tale. Girl gets stranded, the knight in shining armor pulls up with his Channing Tatum good looks, *and* he's interested in what I have to say. Score! I started to feel less anxious about being stranded in the middle of nowhere and thought this was just another experience to add to my book.

As Brady drove me to his father's shop, I couldn't help but glance over, examining him like he was some sort of an investigation. His skin was the perfect color of olive with not a single blemish or flaw. From the side view, I could see his eyelashes looked as if they were covered with mascara. They were perfect. With one arm up on the steering wheel, I was able to see his muscles through the tight-fitted shirt. He wasn't one of those obnoxious-looking gym type guys. He looked more like the kind of man who got muscles from lots of hard labor. I was developing a crush on him that was growing with every passing minute. I forgot all about my broken car, my broken phone, and my broken family.

CHAPTER TEN

We pulled into a driveway with a small building in the front that read, "Buck's Garage." Behind it was an actual garage that fit about four or five cars. It was a smaller place but seemed reputable. As Brady parked the truck he said, "Okay, this is it. Let's see if we can get your car fixed up so you can get back to your trip."

I smiled over at him and got out of the truck. We walked inside the building and I was impressed with the décor, since it was just an auto body shop. It wasn't glamorous but there was what looked like a working jukebox sitting in the corner. There were many pictures hanging on the wall of artists like Johnny Cash and John Denver, so I assumed his father was a big country music fan.

Brady went behind the counter and picked up the telephone. He looked over at me and said, "I'm going to call Mike. He is our tow guy and I'm going to see if I can get him to pick up your car." "Great, thanks," I replied.

While he was making the call, I noticed one of those water jugs some businesses have for clients so I grabbed a cone-shaped cup and began to pour. My throat felt so dry and scratchy from my stressful afternoon. I knew I would have to call home and tell them what happened. My dad would flip out and want me home immediately. How was I going to ever get around this catastrophe?

"Okay, you are all set. Mike is going to go grab your car and we can take a look," Brady said.

"I know I've already thanked you a bunch of times but really, I do appreciate it," I replied.

"Well, it's kind of my job so no need to thank me. Hey, are you by chance hungry?" he asked.

My stomach had been growling and I am one of those stress eaters. I eat whatever I can find when I'm stressed. Chocolate, of course, is always the preference but beggars can't be choosers. "I'm starved actually," I answered.

"There is this little restaurant in town I can take you to if you'd like since it will take awhile till your car is ready," he explained.

I nodded. "Sounds good."

"Okay great, let me just go wash my hands and we can go. Hopefully, by the time we get back, we will have some answers for you," he said.

As Brady went into the back to wash his hands, an older gentleman came out from behind. He noticed me and said, "You must be the traveling girl who is having car problems?"

"That's me," I said with a giggle.

"I'm Buck, and this is my garage. Don't worry, we will have you back on the road in no time. If you need anything at all, just ask Brady."

"He has been overly kind thus far, and I really am grateful for the hospitality," I replied.

"And they say southern hospitality is the best. I think we got them beat," Buck said with a laugh. I liked Buck. He was down-to-earth and quite humorous. I felt as if I've known these people a lot longer than just an hour.

"Okay, you ready Anna?" asked Brady.

He must have cleaned more than just his hands because he looked good. He must have washed his hair because the hat was gone and his hair looked so sexy. Those blonde locks draped over his head and I just wanted to run my fingers through them. I found it rather cute that he dolled himself up for me. And here I was in my ragged old sweatshirt and jeans with a hole in the knee. That used to be the style back in the 90s. As Brady walked beside me, he even smelled delicious.

"Dad, we'll be back shortly. I'm just taking Anna here to get a bite to eat."

"Make sure you order her one of them milkshakes. They're good," Buck said with a giggle.

"I love milkshakes," I said as we walked out of the shop.

"The restaurant is only a few miles up the road. It's a very good place. I think you will like it," Brady said.

"As long as they sell food, I'm sure I'll love it," I replied with a laugh.

"A girl with an appetite, I like that."

"Oh, but I'm definitely not a salad type of girl. Give me a big juicy burger and some greasy fries." As soon as I finished saying "fries," Brady and I both blurted out at the same time, "and a chocolate shake."

And there it was—*love at first milkshake.*

He *knew* me…and at that moment, I craved that milkshake Buck was talking about. I didn't want just any chocolate shake either. It had to be one of those shakes you get at a good diner—the kind that are thick like ice-cream that you can barely suck up through the straw. That's what I was craving.

* * *

We pulled into this very cute and trendy-looking restaurant. It wasn't as small as a diner but it was similar. The sign outside was lit up in pink neon and said, "Donna's." "This is definitely my kind of place," I said to Brady and smiled. He smiled back and said, "Donna has been a friend of the family for a long time. Her parents owned this place and she took it over when they passed away. She's a great lady."

As the doors swung open, I saw a counter with stools, a jukebox in the corner playing 50s music, and some little tables set up all around. I felt like I just walked on to the set of *Grease.* The décor was blue and silver with sparkles in the seats. The pictures on the walls were from the 50s and 60s, I presumed. There was even one of Marilyn Monroe. I loved her.

A waitress with poufy brown hair tied up in a ponytail and wearing a cute little apron came over to us with a big smile. She leaned into Brady and gave him a squeeze. "Brady, so good to see you, handsome," she said.

"It's great to see you too, Marlene," he replied. "This is Anna. Her car is in our shop so I figured I'd better take her for a bite to eat at the best place in town."

"Oh come on now, Brady, this is the only place in town to eat," she laughed as she put her hand out to say hello.

"Anna, it's a pleasure to meet you. There is no one better to show you around this town than this here Brady."

"It's nice to meet you too, Marlene. Brady's been wonderful."

"Okay kids, come this way and I'll sit you at the best table we have."

She took us over by the window, which actually overlooked a little pond they had in the back of the restaurant. There were a few of those walkway lights around it which made it look quite pretty. I also noticed a couple of benches set up around the pond. "That's a cute setup they have back there," I said to Brady.

"Yeah, in the summertime this place has the best ice cream and everyone likes to sit out there and watch the ducks in the pond," he said.

"Are you one of those people who like the ice cream?" I asked.

"Well, I *am* a junk food junkie and ice cream tops my list. I go crazy for mint chocolate chip," he replied with a smile.

"Mint chocolate chip, eh? I'd have to say I'd go for the chocolate chip cookie dough," I said with a laugh.

"Well, then you had better order some because they are known especially for their cookie dough ice cream," Brady responded as he opened the menu.

The menu was also very fifties-themed, with a picture of a red Shelby on the front. As I browsed through the choices my stomach started to growl. What was I going to get? Everything looked so delectable. Did I want the fish and chips? Perhaps a burger would satisfy my hunger. A BLT sounded good too. "What's your favorite thing to get here?" I asked Brady.

"Well, everything is really good, but I always go with the bacon cheeseburger. It's full of grease but so worth it." he replied.

"Okay, a cheeseburger it is," I said. A few moments later Marlene came walking over. "Are you adorable kids ready to order?" she asked.

"Yes, we are," said Brady. He signaled me to go first.

"I'll have the cheeseburger, well-done, with french fries please," I said.

"Okay, so no moo'ing cheeseburger for you," she giggled. She then looked over at Brady and said, "You want your usual?"

"You know it," he replied. "Also, can we get two of Donna's signature chocolate milkshakes with whipped cream on top?"

"Of course you can, but don't go spoiling your dinner now," she said.

"We won't. Thanks Marlene," he said.

"Okay, it'll be about fifteen minutes, so you kids enjoy yourselves," she said as she walked away.

"Milkshake with whipped cream—nice touch," I said to Brady.

"The whipped cream is crucial," he said.

The more Brady opened his mouth to talk, the more I liked hearing him. He told me all about the town and where he grew up. There was something about him that was different from the boys back home. He didn't seem like one of those drunken frat boys. Brady seemed like he had intelligence and respect. The whole time I was with him he was a total gentleman. He reminded me a little of Ryan, except for the fact that I was totally lusting after this guy.

While we were waiting for our food, Brady kept talking. I think that's what I liked about him the most, besides his gorgeous looks. A lot of guys wait for the girl to talk but he seemed very comfortable with himself. It was definitely a turn on. He asked me many questions about my childhood and my family. I was impressed that he wanted to know so much. Then he asked me a question that was deeper than any question a person has ever asked me before.

He asked, "What is your greatest fear in life?"

I thought for a moment, caught off guard. Most people normally ask about your hopes and dreams but this guy wanted to know what I feared. How do I even answer a question like that?

"There are a lot of things in life that I fear. Things like spiders and clowns, but I'm assuming that's not the kind of answer you're looking for."

"Surprisingly, there are lots of people who are afraid of clowns. I'm not, however, I do see the creepy aspect of them." he said.

"I guess I would have to answer that question by saying *time*," I replied.

"Time?"

"Yes. I often worry that I won't have enough time to do all the things I want or say all the things I need to say."

He gazed at me in a way no one ever has and said, "You make perfect sense."

"Since my grandmother died, so much has changed in my life. My family is acting differently and it's hard to grasp. I want to live my life as much as I can for her, for my grandmother. She would want me to be happy and have as many experiences as possible. I only hope that I can take advantage of all that comes my way," I replied.

"Well, I think taking this trip is already one way you are taking advantage, so I don't think you should fear time too much, Anna," Brady said.

Marlene came back with our shakes and food. What was I going to try first? Everything looked so good. I took a bite out of the burger and Brady was right, it had to have been the best burger I've ever tasted. Perhaps it had something to do with the beef being from the Midwest. Whatever the reason, it was delicious.

"How do you like it?" Brady asked.

I wiped the corner of my lip with a napkin and said, "It's the best burger I have ever had."

"I'm glad you're enjoying it," he said.

We both sat there and smiled at each other between bites. In a way, I missed having a boyfriend. It was nice sharing a meal with a guy who made your heart flutter. The beginning stages of a relationship were always the best. You get the butterflies in your tummy and want to make sure you look perfect on every date and you stress over what you will wear. Except in this situation, I didn't have a choice with my clothes. I would have much rather been sporting my skinny jeans and a cute top with black pumps.

As I bit into another fry, Brady opened his perfect mouth and said, "You're really pretty, you know."

I was definitely not expecting those words to come out of his mouth. Didn't he know I was stressing over the horrible outfit I was wearing?

"Thanks, that's very sweet. I sort of feel like a bum in these clothes," I replied.

"I like how you look," he said. "It's nice to have a meal with a girl who's not stressed about her outfit or how her hair looks and if her lipstick is still on. None of that stuff should matter to you because you're pretty without any of it," he said.

I could tell he was a little nervous with his words, hoping he didn't offend me. I thought it was rather sweet and our little meal actually started to feel like a date.

"That's really nice of you to say. It's been awhile since I've even been out to dinner with a guy. With school and everything going on, I've just been too busy. It's nice having dinner with you. And just for the record, I think you are very good looking too. Although I am quite sure you hear it all the time, like when we first walked in the door," I said with a laugh.

He smiled with his big grin and said, "Yeah well, it's nice to hear it from someone new and someone who isn't fifty-three years old." We both laughed as we sipped on our shakes.

"Do you mind if I go check out the jukebox?" I asked.

"I'll go with you. What kind of music do you listen to?"

"Everything. My parents raised me on the older music so I tend to like a lot of the 60s but I still listen to bands like Maroon Five and Bruno Mars. Are you a country boy?"

"I do like country but like you, I listen to everything." He looked over the jukebox with me and then said, "Here, let me play this song for you. I think you will like it, and it reminds me of you with your road trip."

I wondered what song he was going to play. I watched his manly hands press the buttons to play the song. We stood there for a moment as I looked at the title. "Cruise Along?" I asked.

"Yeah, it's this country band called The Georgia Line. Have a listen," he said.

As I listened to the words and watched his lips move as he sang, I suddenly wanted to kiss him. They looked so soft and it had been such a long time since I'd been kissed. I could hear him pipe out some of the words and his voice was amazing.

"Baby, you make me wanna' drive all night and cruise along," he sang. He looked at me and laughed.

"No, don't stop, you're really good," I said.

"Nah, I'm no Adam Levine," he laughed.

"I don't know, you could be," I said.

He put his hand on the middle of my back and said, "Let's go back to the table and finish those shakes before they melt."

In the back of my mind, I knew I had to call home and tell my dad all about this. I couldn't help but enjoy this moment though. For the first time in a long time, I was living. When I felt his hand on me, my entire body trembled. How did this stranger have such an effect on me? I had friends who have had so-called "one-night stands," but this was different. We didn't meet at some bar, completely drunk and sloppy. We both were coherent and it really started to feel like a first date.

We kept blushing and smiling at each other as we drank our shakes. It's not always easy to read people. Sometimes you end up second-guessing whether or not they like you or are just being nice. I was hoping it wasn't just his Midwestern hospitality. Then I found myself getting depressed thinking about the fact that we lived so far away from each other and this was really only a stop along my journey. Yes, many people have long distance relationships and of course there's the Internet, but I like actually seeing and touching a person vs. using technology.

"So tell me more about your family," he asked, that dreadful question.

How do I answer this one, I thought? "Well, they are complicated," I answered.

"All families are complicated," he responded with a smile.

"Yeah, but mine tops the charts for nutty," I laughed.

"What's so nutty about them?" he asked.

"Sometimes I wish I could go back to being a kid. When I was growing up, I didn't notice any of the drama, really, between my family members. I loved them all the same and had a blast every time we all got together. Family parties were the best. I played with my cousins and I felt like it was a decent childhood, with the exception of my mother, of course," I said.

"You don't have a good relationship with your mother?" He looked puzzled.

"I do, but she likes her bottle and pills sometimes. She's actually in rehab as we speak. I don't know how my father deals with it all." I looked down at the table.

"Hey," he said as he leaned over and touched my hand. "We all have our battles, and some are worse than others. On the bright side, she is in rehab, right?"

There was something about his voice, his presence, that calmed me. I wasn't even mad at my mother anymore. I didn't understand her habits but I knew that I had my own life to live now. Brady made me feel like I needed to forgive her in order to move on.

"I used to think she really wasn't trying to get better. She would just pretend she was in order to keep my father around. But you're right and who am I to judge. I guess I turned out alright," I said with a half smile.

"I bet you have a great father," he said.

Every time he opened his mouth, it felt like I'd known him forever. He just seemed to "get" me. I smiled at him and said, "I do, I really do. My dad is a good man and I am lucky he has kept the house together all these years." Brady took a sip of his shake and smiled at me. His deep blue eyes were straight out of a magazine. It was hard not to keep staring into them. "This milkshake is so good but I'm feeling awfully full," I said.

"Well, I'm glad you're enjoying it, considering your car is broken down and you're eating dinner with a complete stranger," he replied.

"The strange thing is, the more I talk to you, the less you feel like a stranger." I smiled and took one last sip of my shake.

"Thank you for that. I will consider that a compliment," he said. "It's been awhile since I've taken a girl out, actually, not that this is the best date place to take someone. Usually, I like to dine a girl at a steakhouse but the closest one is about forty miles away and I didn't want to creep you out or anything by driving that far out."

"That's okay, this place was perfect, and any girl would be lucky if you took her here," I replied blushing. "Have you had any serious relationships?"

He took a deep breath and started to explain. "There was one girl that I dated for over a year. We started out okay but the closer I got to her, the further she drifted. She needed to experience life and fun. I guess I wasn't those things for her." He seemed somber, yet not unhappy.

"I'm sorry to hear that," I replied.

"Don't be. It's important to feel heartaches every now and then to make you appreciate things more."

Was this guy for real? Someone pinch me. Either he was good at fishing for women or he was one in a million. I hate using that term but there wasn't any other way to describe it.

"How about you? You must have had a couple of boyfriends?" he asked.

I sarcastically laughed and said, "I just don't have time for a relationship."

"Come on now, everyone has time for love," he said.

"Everyone but me, I guess," I replied.

"Nah, you have time. The problem is, you haven't met someone worth investing your time with," he explained.

He was right. I hadn't found anyone that even remotely interested me back home. I'd go out with friends and every now and then some random guy would hit on me but it didn't feel right. "The guys where I'm from are not as suave as you," I said flirtatiously.

"Oh, well, not everyone can be like me," he joked.

"You're definitely not like most guys I've talked to lately," I said.

He smiled and said, "Well, I hate to leave but I'm sure you'd like to know what's going on with your car."

Actually, no, I really didn't care at that point what was happening with my car. I could have stayed in that little fifties diner all night long. "Sure, I guess we can go see what the damage is," I replied.

I tried to take money out of my change purse and he said, "Please, allow me to buy you this very cheap meal, especially since your day hasn't gone as you would have liked."

"That's very sweet, and thank you. It hasn't gone my way but honestly, it hasn't been that bad either," I said with a smile. He flashed those baby blue eyes back at me, smiled, and I swear he stole my heart. What a good thief he was.

* * *

On the drive back to the shop we barely spoke a word. The smiles were stretched out cheek to cheek though. I glanced over at him a couple of times and we shared a moment. I wondered what he was thinking. *Did he feel what I was feeling? Was this just a routine thing for him—living out here in the sticks, meeting damsels in distress?* I tried not to think about any of that. I wanted to remember this as a special accident with only good thoughts.

It's like when you meet a guy and you know he's probably had a million women, yet he makes you feel special. You don't want to lose that feeling of standing out among the crowd, even though in the back of your mind you know you're also just a number. That's why I have never had a one-night stand. I prefer letters over numbers anyway. I hear some of my girlfriends talk about their wild nights with the hot guys they take home from the bar. I often wondered if it really was that good. I think some girls just do it so they don't have to go home lonely. I'm not sure I would enjoy a one-nighter, although Brady would be the perfect one to do it with.

While my mind was drifting away, I noticed we were pulling back into Buck's Auto Garage. I wondered what the damage would be. *Would it be fixed and then I'd be on my way and never see or hear from Brady again? It sort of felt like a one-night stand even though we kept our clothes on. I must be crazy.* A part of me wanted to stay longer and had hoped it would take longer for them to fix it. Then I remembered I still hadn't faced that phone call to my dad, and my stomach began to churn.

Brady got out of the truck and came over to my side to open the door. I could get used to this kind of treatment. "Thanks," I said as I jumped out of the truck. As we walked into the reception area, I saw Brady's father talking to the mechanic.

Buck took off his glasses and said, "Anna, the head gasket on your car is busted. Unfortunately, it will be a couple of days before we can get the part. I've called a few places around the area and no one has the part in stock. It has to come direct from the dealer. I'm very sorry."

Now what do I do? I was stranded here in this little town in the middle of nowhere. I looked over and saw Brady standing quietly while I took the news from his dad. That meant I got to stay and spend more time with him. *Everything happens for a reason, Anna,* I told myself. I had no idea how my father was going to take the news.

"Okay, thanks Buck. I guess I better call my father so he doesn't worry," I replied.

"Please, Anna, feel free to use my office phone so you have some privacy. Brady, show her where that is," he said.

"Thanks, I really appreciate it," I replied. I followed Brady into the back where there were some small offices and then a larger one with a nice window and decent furniture.

"Okay, this is it. I'll be waiting in the front for you," Brady said.

As I walked over to the phone, my heart began to race. What would my father say? I really hoped it would go straight into voice mail. I had to explain that I was in a random town, all alone, stranded, with no car and no cell phone. I know I'm twenty-two years old, but it's my dad we're talking about. I picked up the phone and started dialing. With every push of the buttons, I could feel myself getting tense. It was ringing. *Please don't answer, please don't answer.*

"Hello?" said Auntie Sharon. She must have been over visiting with my father.

"Auntie Sharon, hi, it's me, Anna."

"Anna! Hi sweetheart, it's so good to hear your voice. Your father has been worried sick."

"I know, and I'm really sorry about that. I haven't been able to find a replacement yet for my phone."

"That's not good, Anna, especially when you're on the road. What are you going to do?" she asked.

"Well, I'm hoping that as soon as my car gets fixed, I can find a cell phone store," I said nervously.

"Wait, what?" she asked. "Your car is not working? What happened and where are you?" I could hear my father in the background next to her sounding very concerned.

"Well, I was driving along the highway when I heard a noise. I pulled over and the car wouldn't start. Luckily, a very nice gentleman pulled over to help and his father owns a garage, which is where I am now. I am totally fine, I promise," I explained. I could hear my father say, "Let me talk to her, Sharon."

"Anna, what is going on and where are you?" he asked ferociously.

"I'm in a town called Yellow Springs. It's very nice and I am okay, Dad. The head gasket broke in the Civic so it will be a couple of days before it gets fixed because they have to order the part," I replied. He hummed and hawed and I could tell he was frustrated.

"I didn't mind you wanting to get away and take a road trip, Anna, but I am officially concerned that you are a young woman all alone in some place I've never even heard of," he said.

"I know Dad, but you don't have to worry, really."

"I don't have to worry? Anna, you are stranded with no car and apparently no cell phone either. Where are you going to stay?"

"I'm sure there's a hotel around here. I will call you when I get settled into a room. These people have been very hospitable, Dad. I know you're worried, but I'm smart."

"I know you're smart. It's the other people I worry about. The world is not as safe as it once was. I really wish you would just fly home and leave the Civic there," he said.

"Dad, I can't. I came on this trip for a reason and I need to finish what I started. It may be hard for you to understand, but there is something I must do," I replied.

He was quiet for a moment and then asked, "How are you paying for all these expenses? Do you need my credit card number?" Here I was, twenty-two years old, and my dad still wanted to take care of me.

"Dad, don't worry about any expenses. I'm all set. Thank you for asking, and if I need it, I will tell you, I promise," I explained.

"You promise to call me every day and let me know when you're back on the road, right?" he asked.

"Yes, I will, and just to calm your nerves, Dad, I really am enjoying myself."

"Be careful and call me in the morning," he said.

"Bright and early! I love you Dad," I said as I hung up the phone.

A part of me thought I should have asked him about my mother and his visit to Vermont but I'm sure my conversation already doubled the stress on him.

As I walked back out into the shop, I knew Brady was curious to hear how my conversation went.

"All set?" he asked. "Yes, I'm good, other than the fact that I need to find a hotel?" I questioned.

Buck spoke up and said, "Brady, you can take her over to that new little Inn past the pharmacy and tell them we sent her. They will give her a great rate." Buck then looked over at me and said, "You'll like the place, it's very clean and reasonable. Hopefully, we will have your car fixed real soon. I wish we had a rental here but we don't. I can call around tomorrow for you if that's something you want to look into. In the meantime, just call my son if you need anything. He needs to keep busy." I laughed, as did Buck, but I don't think Brady found it to be as funny.

Before we left, I walked to the car to grab my bags so I'd have clean clothes. We then jumped back into Brady's truck and took off. I felt bad that he was like my own personal driver. I offered to pay him some gas money but being the gentleman that he is, he looked at me as if I had five heads. I guess girls in the Midwest aren't as independent as us snooty New England chicks.

Brady and I struck up another interesting conversation about our childhoods. I learned that his father was always a hard-ass. He said that he and his mother had a great relationship and that she was a real sweet lady. I was taught that if a man is good to his mother, he will be good to his woman. That was a rule of thumb that I lived by when it came to dating guys. If they ever told me they didn't have a good relationship with their mother, I backed off. Of course there are always exceptions to every rule. Not all moms are wonderful. Mine was a good example. I wondered how she was doing. I hoped that this time she really was dedicated to getting better. Brady told me he had about twenty first cousins because both his parents had many siblings. I always liked a big family but who can afford them nowadays? College costs are insane. It should be illegal to charge students so much for education.

Brady then told me that his father had always wanted to name his garage "Buck and Sons." "When I confessed that I didn't want to be part owner of the garage, my father's attitude toward me changed drastically," he explained.

"Do you not like working at the garage?" I asked.

"I don't mind it but I don't want it to be my life," he explained. "And I've thought about going to college."

"It's hard when you and your parents don't see eye to eye. I'm sure your dad would love for you to be interested in the garage but you also have to be true to yourself," I said.

"My father laughed when I told him I wanted to be a psychologist. He wondered why I would want to sit around all day and listen to everyone else's problems. He tried to get me interested in the financial world but sitting in a cubicle all day crunching numbers is not my thing. My passion is with people. I am prepared to handle the worst of cases. Some people really live depressing and painful lives. If I can help them, even just a little bit, I will feel grateful," I explained.

"I may call you when I disagree with my father for some therapy," he said with a laugh.

"I would like that," I said with a smile.

When I asked Brady about his siblings, he sort of changed the subject. I wasn't sure what the deal was but I didn't want to push it. People will only share what they feel comfortable sharing and for some reason, he was masking something. Even though he didn't let out all the skeletons from his closet, I learned a lot about him that day, maybe even more than I knew about my own friends back home.

We pulled up to the Inn and Brady got out with me. It looked nice and quaint. The building had pillars in the front and was white with some brick siding. There were walkway lights leading up to the entrance and a small blue lit fountain. I couldn't wait to get in my room at this point. It was a long day. There was a nice fireplace in the lobby with two couches. I could get used to this place. It was very homey.

As we walked up to the reception area, there was a middle-aged man sitting in a chair reading a magazine. It looked like some sort of antique book. "Can I help you?" he said as he stood up and greeted us.

"Yes, I need a room for a night or two for my friend. Her car is being fixed at my father's garage and I was told you would give her the best rate," Brady explained.

It felt good to be taken care of.

"Okay, sir, let me see what I have available," the hotel clerk said as he checked the computer. "I can give her a room with a queen-sized bed and pullout couch, also equipped with a small fridge and a coffeemaker, for the grand total of $67 a night," he said with a half grin.

Brady looked at me to get my approval and I smiled at the hotel clerk and said, "That sounds perfect, thank you very much."

"Okay, I just need a credit card for our files," said the hotel clerk.

I reached into my purse and took out my Visa. "Here you go," I said as I handed it over to him.

"Okay great, let me swipe this in and get you a room key. You are in Room 214, which is right upstairs," he said. I looked over at the staircase and it twirled a bit. *How cute*, I thought to myself. He handed me my key and I grabbed my bags.

"Do you need any help up to the room?" asked Brady. I looked at him, smiled, and said, "I really appreciate all you have done for me today but I think I'm all set. You can go home and actually enjoy the rest of your night."

"What makes you think I didn't enjoy my night?" he asked flirtatiously. "How about I pick you up in the morning around nine-thirty and we can grab some breakfast?"

"Sounds good. I love breakfast and will look forward to that," I replied.

"Okay, well, get some rest and I'll see you in the morning then," he said as he took his keys out of his coat pocket.

I wanted to hug him or kiss his cheek or something but I chickened out. I just turned around and started walking up the twirl staircase with my bags. The cherry wood that covered the railing was exquisite. To stay at a place like this for $67 was a steal.

I found my room and went inside. It was a decent sized room with a nice cozy bed and a couch that faced the flat-screen television. Everything smelled brand new. The bathroom had one of those old style deep tubs. I decided to soak in that for awhile. It was relaxing just lying in the bubbles. I thought about the day and all the events that occurred. I definitely had some stories to share with Chelsea and Ryan when I got back home.

CHAPTER ELEVEN

Beep, Beep, Beep. The alarm was going off already. Why is it that some nights you fall asleep and it seems like you've only had your eyes closed for a minute, then it's time to wake up? I hit the Snooze button, rolled over, and closed my eyes. Five more minutes sounded good to me. The warm sun was shining in on my cheek and it felt good. It reminded me that today was a new day and I needed to make the best of it. I knew Brady would be here soon so I had to get ready. At least this time, I could look halfway decent.

I turned the shower knob on and stepped into the deep tub. I picked up the honeysuckle-scented soap from the Inn. I loved that smell, especially as summer was approaching. As I turned off the water, I could hear the phone ringing. I quickly jumped out and wrapped a robe around me. "Hello?" I answered.

"Anna, it's Brady. I hope you slept well," he asked.

The water was dripping onto the floor as I replied with a smile, "Yes, I slept very well. I'm just getting out of the shower actually."

"Oh, okay, I was going to swing by in about twenty minutes. Does that give you enough time?" he asked.

"Twenty minutes is perfect," I said.

"I will have the front desk call up to you when I arrive," he explained.

"Great, I'll be waiting," I said as I hung up the phone.

Twenty minutes! I had to get moving. I opened up my bag and found a pair of skinny jeans and a cute button-down shirt. I figured I would fit in perfectly with that attire. It was better than the raggedy old clothes I had on yesterday. The bathroom was equipped with a hair dryer, thank God. If I let my hair air dry, it would be a big pouf ball. I pulled out my big round brush and styled away.

Fifteen minutes later, I was ready to go. I decided to meet Brady downstairs in the lobby so I grabbed my purse and headed down the stairs. I sat on one of the couches by the fireplace to wait for him. There were a few magazines on the coffee table. I found one that gossips about all the stars so I picked it up to read. Half of the time those stories were all a bunch of bullshit but like many consumers, I enjoyed it. As I flipped through some of the pages, I noticed Brady entering the Inn. He had on a nice pair of jeans, some new sneakers, and a black T-shirt that fit well against his chiseled body. As he approached me I noticed he was wearing cologne. It was a fresh scent and it drew me in.

I stood up to greet him. "Hi, thanks so much for coming to get me."

He smiled and said, "No problem. It gets lonely eating breakfast alone so I welcome the company. Are you ready to go?" he asked as he held out his arm for me to wrap mine around. It was the kind of thing they still did in Europe and it was nice. I slid my arm through his and we walked out of the Inn.

"What did you think of the place?" Brady asked.

"It was very nice and charming. Thank you for getting me such a good rate."

"That was my dad's idea," he said with his gorgeous smile.

This little town of Yellow Springs was growing on me. When I think about how awful I felt when my car broke down to now going to breakfast with this amazing guy, I realize that life surely wasn't all that bad.

"The place I am going to take you for breakfast is this cool little café, much better than your normal Starbucks," he said with a laugh.

"Well, I am more of a Dunkin' girl anyway. Do you have any around here?"

"The closest Dunkin' Donuts is about twenty miles away. They proposed one in town here a few years back but the mayor frowned upon it because he didn't want small business to suffer. We take pride in our small business operations around here. Everything is getting so commercialized," he explained.

"The charm of a town is based upon its people and the workers. It's refreshing to know there are still towns like this in America—while I do love Dunkin', the small café sounds perfect this morning," I said to Brady with a smile.

We drove for about ten minutes. "There it is," he said, pointing to a little place in the shape of a coffee cup.

"Are you kidding me? The place was actually built to look like a coffee cup? How cool is that?" I said.

"It is very cool. I figured you would like it. I don't want you to leave here thinking we have nothing to offer," Brady said.

I looked over at him. "Every minute I spend around here, I see great offerings."

He smiled back, almost blushing. I think he understood my flirtatious comment but guys don't always read our minds. We parked in a small parking lot behind the coffee cup and walked around to the front.

The café was pretty cool and much neater than any Starbucks I'd ever seen. On one side there were two couches facing each other and a fireplace to add to the ambiance. On the other end there were a couple of tables and some computers set up for guests to use. There were also some counters and stools set up in between for patrons just stopping in for a quick snack or cup of coffee.

"Where would you like to sit?" he asked.

"Those couches look pretty cozy, unless you'd rather sit at a table," I said.

"Couches will be great. Let's go order." He took my arm and guided me over to the cashier.

Brady ordered a blueberry coffee and a macaroon. I decided to get the banana chocolate chip muffin and an Irish cream coffee. As he was reaching in his pocket for his wallet, I had already given the cashier a twenty I had in my pocket. "Please, let me buy you breakfast," I said. "It is the least I can do for you." He smiled and said thank you.

We took our seats on the couches and put our coffees on the table. The warmth from the fireplace felt great even though it was late spring.

"I love the sound of a crackling fire," I said to Brady.

He took a sip of his coffee and said, "You'd like my house then because we always have a fire going. We even have huge bonfire parties all through the summer."

"Bonfires are the best," I replied. "It's fun to just chill and drink a beer with your friends."

"So you are a beer girl, eh? I sort of had you pinned for a red wine drinker, seeing you're from Connecticut," Brady said.

"A wine girl? Is that what most people think of Connecticut girls? That we're all stuck up and rich?" I asked with a laugh.

He laughed back and replied, "Sort of, we do. But you clearly are making me see things differently. If all the girls in Connecticut are as cool as you, I may have to come visit."

"I will take that as a compliment and you are welcome to come visit me anytime in New England. I can be your personal tour guide. It is, after all, the least I can do," I said.

"So what are the perceptions about Midwestern guys?" he asked curiously.

"Oh, we think they're just farm boys who chew tobacco and smoke ten packs a day," I laughed and took a sip of my coffee.

"Ten packs a day?" he said with a surprise. "I think seven is our limit, although I don't fit your mold of Midwestern guys too well because I don't smoke, nor do I have a green thumb to save my life."

"I don't have a green thumb either. Whenever someone buys me a plant, I end up giving it to my Aunt Sharon because it would never last in my house. I like the fake stuff. Looks great and easy to maintain," I said.

We continued to talk about college and our friends and family again. Before both of us realized it, we had been sitting in that little coffee cup place for over two hours. I had told him all about our crazy family parties but mostly about my grandmother. I loved talking about her. It seemed to keep her alive in so many ways. I think people are sometimes afraid to talk about those who have passed for fear of bringing up sad thoughts. It is the opposite for me. If someone had played such an important role in your life, whether it is a mother, father, grandparent, or even a child, you want to speak of them often because doing so makes it seem as if they are still with you.

Brady asked me if he could take me somewhere. He didn't tell me where or what we'd be doing, but so far everything we had done together was fun so I accepted. We left the coffee place and once again hopped into his truck.

"Now, don't panic because where I am going to take you is a little bit off the beaten path," he said. *Off the beaten path*, I thought. That's the good thing about knowing locals when you travel. They always seem to know where the good spots are, whereas most tourists drive right by without ever knowing the beauty that remains.

He drove the truck off the road on a dirt path. It was a path people used for four-wheeling or something. It made me feel better knowing other people must have been on this road.

"I used to come out here all the time," he said.

"Why did you stop?" I asked. He sort of stalled to answer, and then said, "It's a bit of a long story but I'll share it with you when we get there."

Branches were swiping against the sides of his truck but I don't think he minded. It wasn't a brand new vehicle but I know some guys who obsess over their cars.

Through all the brush, we came out to a place that looked like some sort of make out cliff straight out of a movie. I had to admit, it was quite beautiful. "Wow, this place is amazing," I said.

"Sometimes when you go off the beaten path, you find something more valuable," he said.

When he spoke, he sounded poetic. He definitely wasn't cut out for the automobile industry. He was a smart guy but he had so much more to offer with the use of his words. He said he told his father once that he wanted to be a writer. Of course his father didn't take that too well because of the garage. Parents like to tell us what to do even as we get older because they want us to succeed and live comfortably.

We got out of the truck and he grabbed a blanket for us to sit on. We hopped into the back of the truck with our legs dangling down.

"The mountains look beautiful. I thought it was all flatland around here," I said.

"You can't always judge a book by its cover," Brady said as he looked down at his feet.

I could tell something was on his mind. He looked like he wanted to talk about it but was having a hard time. "Everything okay?" I asked.

"My brother died two years ago," he said.

"Oh, I'm sorry," I replied sadly.

Brady got down off the truck and started telling me about it. "His name was Cole. He was a year younger than me but much more intelligent. Cole graduated from high school early so he could go to work with my father. He always worked harder than me and wanted to help run the garage."

Brady was having a difficult time sharing all this but I knew he had to get it off his chest. I could tell it had been bothering him, probably ever since Cole died.

"When I told my father I wasn't that interested in the garage, he flipped on me. He said it should have been you in that car, not Cole. He died in a car crash with one of our close friends. They were going out celebrating someone's twenty-first birthday. Cole never went out. He barely drank alcohol and was a real good guy. It just so happened that I stayed at the shop late that night to work on another friend's car. I was going to meet up with them later at the local bar we hung out at. The worst part was neither one of them were drunk. A drunk driver hit them—smashed right into the passenger side and Cole died at the scene. Our friend Sawyer died at the hospital a few days later from brain trauma," Brady explained as he wiped a tear from his eyes.

I couldn't believe Brady just shared all of that with me. It was like he trusted me enough to open himself up. "I'm sorry your father said that to you, Brady. He didn't mean it. Sometimes when we don't get our own way we compare people and it's not okay, but we're human," I said.

"No, he definitely meant it or was at least thinking it," Brady said.

"I think your father was disappointed that you weren't as motivated about the garage as your brother Cole was, but that's just it, you are not Cole. It's awful what happened and I'm sure your family is still dealing with the pain every day. You are an amazing guy. I barely know you, yet you have been so kind to me. Your parents did a great job raising a good man," I said. Brady was getting choked up and I felt badly for him and his guilt. I wished I could help him.

"Cole and I used to come here. As kids we would ride our bikes, then our dirt bikes, and when we got licenses, we'd come here with friends. I haven't been able to come here since he died."

I got down off the truck and walked over to him. I gently put my hand on his back and said, "Thank you for taking me here."

He smiled and said, "After you shared so much of your life with me in this little bit of time, I thought this would be the best way to show you who I am."

"I can see why you liked coming here. I know it's hard for you, but you should come here and remember Cole and the fun times you did have. It's okay to feel sad or even cry. It's natural and he meant something to you."

Brady took a deep breath and put his arm around me. "Thank you. I don't know how long it would have taken me to come back here if it weren't for you," he said.

I smiled and said, "Tell me about the craziest thing the two of you ever did together?"

"The craziest thing, eh? Well, we've done a lot of crazy stuff together but if I could share just one, it would have to be in the summer of '96. Cole and I were so bored one afternoon, we went to the local department store. We started browsing and walked by these frogs in the garden department. We noticed when you walk by them that they croak. There were about twenty of them so we grabbed a carriage and piled them all in the cart. The store was busy so no one really noticed our frog obsession. As we walked through the store, we placed a frog in different areas. So when people walked by, you would keep hearing the croaks all through the store. When we were done, we just kind of walked around and enjoyed the show. Then we were approached by security. They had rewound the store video to see what Cole and I were doing. We had to walk around the whole store and gather up all the frogs and put them back. We decided on the way out that we were going to buy one. It still sits in our garden at home. That has to be the dumbest, yet funniest thing we did," he said and laughed.

"Sometimes it's the stupidest things we do that are the funniest. What a great story. Thank you so much for sharing that. I think it's really cool that you still have one of the frogs," I replied.

"I'm glad your car broke down," he said.

I looked up at him and whispered, "Me too."

Brady then leaned in and I could feel his lips touch mine. It wasn't one of those gross messy tongue kisses where you feel like the guy is trying to swallow your whole face. It was sweet and innocent. It was the perfect kiss in the perfect location with the perfect guy. It lasted about seven seconds and I would have kept going but I think he didn't want to seem like he was coming on too strong. That's what I liked about Brady. He gave me a little at a time and in return it made me want more.

"You have soft lips," he said as he slowly peeled his lips from mine.

"You can take comfort in them anytime you'd like," I replied.

"I would want them all the time then," he said with a flirty smile.

"So I guess I'll have to come back and visit then."

He looked a bit sad and said, "Yeah, I forgot about that part. You'll be leaving here soon. We should go stop by the garage and see if the part came in yet, but I have to stop home first, if you don't mind. I told my mother I would grab a gallon of milk on the way back through."

"Sure, that's okay. I'd like to meet your mother," I said.

"She will love you," he replied as he opened the truck door for me.

* * *

In some way, I was hoping the part was not in yet. I know I still had a long way to go to research the news in Indiana but I was developing feelings for this guy. We made more small talk on the way over to his house.

"I really want to move out of my parent's house. There is this cool older house that's a bit run down that I'd like to fix," he said.

"At least you have a plan. I need to find a job first before I can think about being on my own. With all that is going on with my mother, I feel it's my responsibility to make sure my dad is okay. He knows how to cook and clean but I feel bad for him," I replied.

"Yeah, that's tough," he said. "It's also why I stay home still. With Cole gone, I felt bad leaving my mom."

Brady stopped into a little convenience store to pick up the milk for his mother. As he was walking toward the store, I kept staring at him. He was perfect and he didn't even know it. I felt bad for him carrying around all that guilt and pain from his brother's death. I then thought about his mother and wondered how she handled the loss of a child. I don't have kids but I can only imagine how deeply it hurts to lose a child. If I ever have children, I hope to God I never outlive them. I was much too sensitive to handle those types of situations. During one semester in college, I visited a children's hospital as part of my case study, and I cried all the way home. To see those little faces smiling at you, knowing they were all sick, and many dying from cancer, and then to see the parents being so strong, was absolutely heartbreaking. That was an area I don't think I could work in. Hospice has a psychologist on staff for the families but I wouldn't be strong enough to help them get through that. I would be mourning with them.

As Brady came out of the store, I saw someone call over to him. It was a girl about our age. She gave him a big hug and it looked like she didn't want to let go. I can't say I blamed her. She spoke with him for about a minute and he said goodbye as she walked into the store. He got back into the truck and let out a big sigh.

"I hate when I see people I really don't want to see."

"An old girlfriend?" I asked.

"Not really. We went on a couple dates after high school but she went off to college in Illinois and became a bit psycho," he explained.

"College can do that to a person," I said laughing.

He put the milk in the backseat and drove off. "I must warn you about my mother," he said. "She is the sweetest lady but she can be over the top sometimes. She likes to hug and kiss people."

I laughed and said, "Well I like her already then. My mother is the opposite and only shows affection to her bottles of Patron."

"At least she has good taste in Tequila," Brady said jokingly.

"Oh, there is no doubt that Patron is a very smooth drink. I just don't think I would fall asleep on the couch cuddled up to it," I replied.

We pulled down a path that ended up being his driveway. "Wow, you are really set off the road," I said.

"We have eleven acres so it's a lot of yard work," he said.

It was a very nice country house with a wraparound porch. Off to the side I could see a woman sitting in a garden. It must have been his mother.

"There's Mom, hard at work in her garden," Brady said.

"Awe, she looks so sweet," I said as we both got out of the car.

Brady grabbed the milk and we walked over toward his mother. When she noticed us she stood up quickly and smiled. "Hi there," she said so sweetly.

"Mom, this is Anna, the girl I told you about last night."

I reached my hand out to her and she shook it with such warmth. "It's nice to meet you. You have an amazing son."

"Oh, aren't you adorable and so sweet, and please call me Laura," she said.

I was happy to hear Brady say he told his mother about me. I don't think many guys like talking to their moms about girls they date.

"Let's go in the house and have ourselves a snack. I just made these little truffles," Laura said.

Brady and I followed his mom into the house. When I walked through the back door, the scent of pumpkin spice hovered in the air. The kitchen was decorated with country décor, straight out of a magazine. As he put the milk away in the fridge, I noticed the charming little breakfast nook. Brady's mom told us to have a seat on the bench at the table and she would get us a little something to eat. I was feeling a bit full from the muffin I had but I always had room for truffles.

"These are chocolate truffles and here are some cookies if you'd like," she said as she put the plate of goodies down in front of us. She then went into the fridge and took out a jug of iced tea. "Do you like iced tea, Anna?"

"Love iced tea," I said as she poured me a glass. We all sat down at the table and enjoyed the treats she made. "These truffles are delicious."

"Why thank you, Anna. I will send you home with a little bag of them. I made about a hundred."

"Wow, thanks so much."

"Hey Mom, have you heard from Dad at all today? I was

wondering if the part came in for Anna's car yet?" Brady asked as he took a bite of a cookie.

"Actually, your dad called about an hour ago and said when he talked to the man at the Honda place, he told him they would have it in by Friday. I think he put a rush on it so it may be here sooner," she replied.

"End of the week?" Brady said a bit surprised. He looked over at me. "Anna, I am so sorry. I'm sure there's something else we can do."

"Your father did say that he was looking into a rental car so she can continue on with her trip. Then she can stop back in Yellow Springs to pick up her car on her way back home to Connecticut."

"I'm sure something will work out," I said as I took another truffle from the plate. "I am quite enjoying this part of my trip, spending time with nice people like you."

"What a kind thing to say, Anna. You are welcome back here anytime. Brady, maybe you can take Anna for a walk and show her the property," Laura suggested.

Brady wiped his mouth with a napkin and said, "Yeah, I will, Mom."

As we walked outside to the back of the house, there was Laura's garden, and I noticed she also had a clothesline. It reminded me of my grandmother's house because she was one of the few people on the street who still hung clothes out to dry. She used to say there was nothing better than pure sunshine drying your clothes.

Brady's parents had a nice home with landscaping that should be featured in a garden magazine. You could tell they enjoyed being outdoors. There was also a small flower garden on the other side of the vegetable garden and a nice round rock wall with a wishing well in the middle. It was surrounded by daffodils, marigolds, and gladiolus. Gladiolus was my grandmother's favorite flower. I liked seeing things that reminded me of her. "Your mother keeps busy around the house, eh?" I asked Brady.

"Yeah, she does. She enjoys being outdoors and takes great pride in her gardening. Her father was a huge garden connoisseur."

"A garden connoisseur, huh? I don't think anyone in my family is considered to be one of those," I said with a laugh. We walked further into the back of the yard toward a little path into the woods.

"You feel like a little hike?" he asked. "Sure," I replied.

He then said to me, "It keeps my mom's mind off of her illness."

His words took me by surprise. First he tells me about the tragic loss of his brother and now his mom was ill? "Your mom's illness?" I asked, confused.

"She was diagnosed with breast cancer six months ago," he explained.

"Oh Brady, I don't know what to say. I almost feel angry that this horrible illness can affect a lovely person like your mom," I said with tears in my eyes.

"She will hopefully be cancer-free after this last chemo treatment she went through. My mom opted to get a mastectomy as soon as she became aware of the diagnosis. She didn't want to take any chances. They gave her chemo afterward, just to be on the safe side."

At that moment, I realized that every family has their tribulations. So far, this day had been kind of depressing and hard on him. I wanted to hug all of his pains away. He was strong, much stronger than I was, to be handling all of this. My mom was in rehab and his almost died.

"Brady, I know that telling you I'm sorry doesn't help much but I really am truly sorry. It sounds like you have had a real rough time lately. Here I was venting about my family back home when meanwhile, you've been dealing with much worse."

"Please don't think that," he said. "Your problems are important to you and we all have our own way of dealing with things. I didn't want to share the sadness of my life because this trip is about you and your family, not mine."

I took his hand. "But it *is* also about you. I know we haven't known each other long but I already care deeply for you. Your family has welcomed me and shown me hospitality that has gone above and beyond. Whatever this is between us, it's rare, and I'm feeling blessed to have met you."

With a tear streaming down his cheek, he pulled me to his chest and held me. I never felt a hug like that before, especially coming from a man. I could feel the emotional bond between us. Maybe that was God's plan. Perhaps he wanted us to meet, if only to find comfort in each other. As I stood there in Brady's embrace, I hoped he would never let go. His arms held me so tight that it gave me this sense of trust that I hadn't felt with any boy before. How was it possible that I've only known this person for two days? It seemed impossible but it was really happening. I felt a tear drop from my eye and land on Brady's shirt.

Brady looked down at me and saw my tears. "Is something wrong?"

I wiped my eyes and said, "No, that's just it, nothing is wrong."

He looked puzzled. "Then why your tears?"

I shrugged my shoulders and said, "I'm just scared." I could feel the tears filling up inside my eyes again. I didn't want this to be a sad moment because it was so perfect.

"Anna, what are you afraid of?" Brady asked as he helped wiped the tears off my cheek.

I took a breath and tried to answer him without breaking down too much. I didn't want to seem like a crazy person. "It's just that this… what we have right now, is so wonderful. It was unexpected, and although I've put my head into school and a career and my family, I've missed out on being in love. Spending time with you makes me realize what I've been missing. It scares me because I'm just on a road trip and I live four hundred miles away."

Brady sort of smiled and with a cute boyish laugh, he sang, "Well, I would walk five hundred miles just to be the man to make you feel this way."

How did he always know what to say? I hugged him tightly and again couldn't believe that God made a man this amazing.

"Listen Anna, I'm just as scared as you are. Us guys, we don't show it as much. Although, you've already seen me *cry* and I think the last time anyone has seen that was when I was six and I fell out of a tree."

I laughed as I continued to wipe my tears and said, "You fell out of a tree?"

He laughed and said, "My brother and I were trying to build a tree house and at six, you don't think about how to make it, you just build it. So I went to sit in the new tree house we had constructed so awesomely and not only did I fall out of it, but the whole house came tumbling down after me."

"Oh, you poor guy, did you get badly hurt?" I asked.

"Just a couple scratches, but after that I learned how important it is to do a job right. So what this is, between us, I want to do it right so neither one of us ends up with any scratches, okay?" he said as he stroked his fingers through my hair.

He looked out at the open field for a moment and then turned to me and said, "Let me take you to Indiana. Think of it as me being your personal chauffeur. I will take you where you need to go. I won't get in the way of you finishing what you started with this adventure. You need answers, and I could use a break from this place."

I looked back at him with surprise and awe that he would even offer something like that. I smiled at him and replied softly, "Are you sure you want to do that?"

"I've never been more sure in my entire life. You inspire me. I feel alive again and I don't want to lose this feeling, not now anyway. So what do you say? Will you let me drive you to Portland?"

It felt as if it were some sort of proposal. With butterflies flying all around my insides, I simply replied, "Yes."

He threw his arms around me again and said, "It will give us more time to get to know each other and figure things out. Not to mention I would feel better if I were with you, just in case. I don't like the sound of a female driving across the country alone, especially a female that I am starting to have crazy feelings for."

I looked up into his eyes and kissed his perfectly proportioned lips.

"If you keep kissing me like that, we won't be going anywhere, Anna," he said to me with that boyish smile.

"You're right," I answered. "It's sort of becoming an addiction of mine and I apologize."

He laughed and said, "Please don't ever lose that addiction, I think it's good for both of us. Come on. Let's go get some things packed for this trip so you can finish what you started."

CHAPTER TWELVE

Brady dropped me off at the Inn so that I could get my things and rest for a few hours. "By the time we come back from Indiana, I promise your car will be ready," he said as I stood outside his truck window. I leaned in a bit and said, "I know it will, but I'm not so sure I will want to leave."

Brady then leaned in and kissed my forehead. I loved it when a guy kissed my forehead. I watched his truck drive out of the parking lot. Even though he would be back soon, I already missed him. I had decided to call home when I got back to my room. I could feel my cheeks still red from blushing. I picked up the room phone and dialed home.

"Dad, it's me, Anna."

"Anna, hey, I am glad you called. What's going on?" he asked with much concern in his voice.

"My car is still in the shop but it's in good hands. They're giving me a rental to use so I can finish my trip and by the time I return to come home, it will be ready." I felt bad lying again but if I told my father that I was letting a boy drive me around the country, he would flip out.

"A rental, eh? I know you're responsible, Anna. I just want you to get your cell phone fixed so that I can get a hold of you. Promise me that it will be the first thing you do as you venture out. Buy a Go-Phone if you have to as I don't want you on the road without any communication."

"Dad, I promise I will have communication on the road. I am going to leave in the morning and will call you by lunchtime tomorrow."

I could still sense some worry over the phone as I hung up with him. I hope my future husband will be just as good to my daughter as my father has been to me. All I could think about was how badly I wanted my mother to change and be the wife my father deserved. I decided to take another bath in the deep relaxing tub. When I move out, I was definitely getting one of these tubs.

Seven-thirty a.m. came early. I packed my bags and headed downstairs to meet Brady. I grabbed us two coffees from the lobby and I met him outside at his truck.

"Thanks for the coffee," he said as he threw my bags in the back seat.

"Well, I might as well get *something* from the free continental breakfast," I replied as I climbed inside his truck.

He must have just gotten out of the shower as his hair was still wet and his scent made me want to jump his bones. Normally, I'm not that kind of girl but something has definitely come over me. For the first time in my life I felt as though someone else had control over my body. At that point, I don't think there was anything I wouldn't do for this boy. It was exciting and scary at the same time.

"Next stop, Portland, Indiana," he said as he looked over smiled.

I wanted to keep him forever. I constantly had to remind myself to slow down. I never believed in love at first sight. It was always hogwash to me. How could people really be in love when they barely knew each other? I knew it was just lust but was there a possibility that I was falling in love? As I gazed over at Brady's profile, I thought there was no way I would ever lose the lust I had for this boy. I was totally infatuated. I tried to hide that part so I didn't seem over-eager. Boys like a chase, so I knew it was important to keep running but with him, it would definitely be at a slower pace. After all, if he can't catch me, what fun would it be? He has been so honest and up front with me since I met him. Maybe he wasn't like those East Coast boys who get bored once they catch their prey. I swear, the college boys were worse than the high school ones. The only boy I had any respect for back home was Ryan.

"I brought some snacks for the trip but we can stop anytime you get hungry," Brady said.

"You are so cute and thoughtful," I replied flirtatiously.

"Well, actually, I don't want to take all the credit. My mom really likes you and told me it would be chivalrous to pack some things," he said with his adorable smile.

"Well, the feeling is definitely mutual, as I think your mom is amazing."

He laughed to himself, making me wonder what he was thinking. Then he said, "My mom never really liked the girls I brought home. I didn't bring home many because there haven't been a whole lot. Even the friends I brought over, my mom never warmed up to. I guess she likes New England girls better than the Midwest girls."

I had to start singing so I belted out, "I wish they all could be New England girls..."

Brady laughed and asked surprisingly, "You can sing?"

I started to shy up and said, "No, not really. I don't like to sing in front of anyone—only in the shower."

He was hesitant to respond but finally he came out with, "Well, I guess I'll have to make an exception and join you in the shower then."

I knew right then and there my face was as bright as a tomato. How do I reply to that one? Of course I wanted to take a shower with him. I could only imagine how amazing that would be. From the looks of it, he had a perfect farm-boy body, with muscles in all the right places. Give me a man in ripped jeans, a flannel shirt unbuttoned, and some cowboy boots. *What was happening to me?* Perhaps I was hitting my peak or maybe it was the fact that I haven't been with a man in over a year. As I was thinking all of these thoughts in my head, he opened that sweet mouth of his again.

"Bad idea? Look Anna, I was totally kidding. Please don't think I expect anything. I'm a respectful guy who cracks a lot of jokes. Not that taking a shower with you would be a joke, but I don't want to make you uncomfortable."

"I'm not uncomfortable. I have a confession to make. After you mentioned the shower thing, I sort of played it out in my head." I quickly covered my mouth. *Oh my gosh, did I just say that out loud?*

Brady had a huge smile and also began to get red.

"I can't believe I just said that," I said with embarrassment.

He laughed and said, "Anna, it's okay. It's human nature. Anytime you want to take a shower with me, you just say the word. I'm real good at washing hair, just so you know."

Okay, now it was getting hot in that truck. I had to roll the window down and I think he knew why. "So what do you have for snacks?" I asked.

He laughed once again and said, "Quenching your desires with snacks—my kind of girl. On a serious note, I have everything in that bag, from fruit to homemade cookies, especially baked for you."

"Well I have to have a cookie then," I replied. I grabbed two cookies from the container and he looked over at me as I took a bite.

"You're so cute to watch," he said. "Can you please stop being so cute so I can drive?"

"Oh, sorry, I will look out the window and enjoy the other beautiful things from this side of the truck." We both laughed and were silent for a while. "Oh, I need to stop at a store that either sells cell phones or where I can get mine fixed because I promised my father I would," I explained.

"Sure, we can do that. There are a few places about thirty miles ahead," he said.

"Perfect. Have I told you how much I appreciate you?" I asked Brady.

"Yes, don't worry, you have. I'm glad to help such a beautiful woman."

I never got tired of hearing him say I was beautiful. When you are not in a relationship or when you have been with someone for a long time, you don't hear simple words like "you're beautiful" that much. It was nice to hear, especially coming from such a gorgeous guy. A part of me wanted to bring him home with me to Connecticut, but another part of me was fearful that every single girl in the state would want him. I was never the jealous type so I must really like this guy.

"We have about six hours to drive and should be in Portland," Brady said. "So, tell me more about your dad? You seem really close to him?"

I smiled as I was glancing out of the truck window. "My dad is a really great guy. You know those movies or shows on TV where the parents seem so perfect? Well, my dad fits that mold. He never yells, just raises his voice. He cooks and cleans and works really hard."

"He sounds great. What does he do for work?" Brady asked.

"He's an actuary for a large insurance company in Hartford. But his real love is carpentry. He's made so many pieces of furniture in our house, like our end tables and coffee tables, and even our bed frames. His work is really exquisite. I'm shocked he never opened his own business instead of working in insurance."

"Having your own business is pretty stressful and when you have a family you have to be careful. He probably put his family first because an actuary is a really good, stable job. With owning a business he knew that it would be a gamble. I'm sure his woodworking is phenomenal because he sure can make beautiful children. In all seriousness, he was probably thinking that if he had his own company and it flopped, his family would suffer," Brady explained so intently.

"You're probably right. Your dad seems to have a great business though," I said.

"He definitely does, and it was actually his father's so he took it over when my grandpa got too old to run it. However, there was a time when business was really slow and we almost lost it. We had to borrow money from my grandparents just to keep up the mortgage, but luckily my dad found a way to turn it all around. I think that's partly why he's mad that I don't want to take over the business. He worked so hard to keep it going," Brady said.

"I understand. That's a really tough place to be in. On one hand you're lucky to have such a great opportunity, but on the other hand you need to live your life so how do you make all parties happy?" I asked.

"There were days I felt like I should just make him happy and take it over, especially with everything that happened with my brother and my mom," Brady said.

"Yeah, but that wouldn't be fair to you. There has to be someone who would want to continue the business."

"Actually, there is. My friend Mike would love it. He's been working for my dad since he was about 14. His parents struggled with bills so my dad gave him a job. He's taught him everything he knows and I think he'd be the perfect owner."

"Have you mentioned this to your dad at all?" I asked.

"No, it's never been the right time. Whenever we discuss the business, he just rants about how I'm a part of the family and with that comes responsibilities," he explained.

"But this isn't about being responsible. In fact, I think you *are* being very responsible. What happens if you took the business over and became miserable and it went belly-up? Wouldn't he rather have someone who is passionate about it so it thrives?" I asked.

Brady looked over at me with a smile and said, "Maybe I'll let *you* talk to my father."

I laughed and said, "If I talk to him about it, he may ban you from the family which means you won't have any place to go, which then means you will have to come back to Connecticut with me."

Brady then replied, "I think it's the perfect plan!"

We drove for awhile, talking about anything and everything. I learned that Brady wasn't much into sports but liked watching football. He was a Browns fan. When I told him I liked the Chicago Bears, he couldn't understand how. I explained that my grandparents had this football helmet in their closet. I could have sworn it was the Bears so I just became a Bears fan. He said he played a little basketball in middle school but it wasn't for him. "Any free time I had, I normally would just write," he said.

"What kinds of things did you write?" I asked.

"When I was younger I pretended to be one of those travel writers so I would research a place in the U.S. and the write about it. If anything, I learned a lot about many different places."

"I think you should do that," I said.

"What?" he asked.

I looked at him with the most serious look and said, "Be a travel writer. The words you speak to me are filled with such passion that I know you would make a great writer."

He smiled at me and said, "Thanks. No one has ever put that much faith in me in so little time before."

"I have a feeling your mom has lots of faith in you. I think your dad does too. He is just too proud to admit it."

Talking to Brady was like talking to Chelsea. I felt I could tell him anything. I tried not to share too much because I didn't want to overload him. Time was limited for us but I didn't want to share my entire life in only a few days. If this road trip romance was going to be something more, I had to let it work itself out. There were times when we needed to have a little faith in life and see where it would take us.

"There is a little shopping mall up ahead in about two miles. We can grab a bite to eat and get you that phone if you'd like?" Brady suggested.

"That's perfect, thanks so much." We pulled off the exit and into a small little mall area with a few restaurants and a Target. "I'm in Heaven," I shouted. "I haven't seen a Target for about two hundred miles."

Brady laughed at me and said, "I'm glad I brought you right up to Heaven. I have that effect on women."

I smacked his arm flirtatiously, "I already know you do."

He pulled into the parking lot and asked, "Where would you like to eat? We have a Marty's, a Denny's, Golden Corral, or a Ruby Tuesday?"

"I'll take the Ruby Tuesday if that works for you?" I asked.

Brady pulled his truck into a spot in front of Ruby's and said, "I was hoping you'd pick that."

As we walked into the restaurant I headed straight for the Ladies Room. I felt as if my bladder was going to explode. The bathrooms were pretty nice and had tasteful décor. They had those pretty bowl-type sinks and the mirror had jewels on the border. As I washed my hands, I looked at myself in the mirror. Something seemed different about me. I couldn't quite figure it out. My hair was the same, my eyes were still greenish yellow, and my lips were shiny from my lip gloss, yet I appeared different. Maybe it was a Brady effect, or that I felt more independent out here in Ohio without my family. I dried my hands under one of those intense dryers that make your skin look floppy, and headed back to the table. Brady was looking over the menu when I sat down across from him.

He handed me a menu and said, "I ordered us some waters and the salad bar to start."

"Thank you, I'm parched and starving, so that works."

The waitress then came over with her great big smile and asked what we would like to eat. I was having one of those moments where I didn't know what I was in the mood for. He ordered Buffalo wings and a beer, typical guy.

"I'll have the Honey Barbeque Chicken Fingers and a side of rice," I finally decided as I handed her the menu.

"Great choice, the Honey Barbeque Chicken is my favorite," the waitress said as she winked at me and left our table.

Brady laughed and said, "I think I may have some competition. The waitress seems to like you."

"A little competition never hurt anyone," I flirted back as I sipped my water.

We exchanged small talk while waiting for our food to arrive. Getting the salad bar was a great idea, otherwise we would have been waiting a long time to eat. They seemed to move at a slower pace out here in the Midwest compared to the East coast. Everything is more rushed in New England. People rush to go nowhere. It's probably why we are labeled as rude. The more laid-back lifestyle was growing on me. Reminded me of the South where they seem less stressed. It was refreshing and for once I was learning how to relax.

"I've thought about going to school on the East coast," Brady blurted out.

As I took a bite of my chicken, I almost choked on it. I looked up at him to see what else he was going to say.

"I applied to Boston University a year ago and was accepted. I never enrolled because of everything going on at home. It makes me feel resentful."

I sat quietly as he gathered his thoughts to share.

"I know it was important to stay and help my family. It's another reason why I convinced myself to take this trip with you. I needed an escape, and meeting you made me realize that. Your car breaking down was a wake-up call. You inspire me, Anna Corolla."

"Me? Thank you for saying that, but I hardly think I am anyone's inspiration. I'm a mess myself, which is why I drove out here to begin with," I said.

"What if you handed that note to your father? Would he do anything with it? Would anyone in your family for that matter?"

He had a good point. I looked him in the eye and then looked down at my half-eaten plate. "I don't know. I didn't think much myself before jumping in my car to drive here. I just knew I had enough of the chaos around me. What if I see this cousin and she tells me news I'd rather not hear?"

"What if she tells you something meaningful?" he debated back. "That's just it. We never know anything until we do it. I can't live in Yellow Springs anymore and keep wondering what it would be like to do things. I need to get up and do them—just like you, Anna."

I smiled at him with as much admiration as a woman could possibly have. I raised my glass of water and said, "Cheers, then—to us —that from now on, we will take chances and never forget what it feels like to be alive." Our glasses clinked as we took a sip of our water.

"I never toasted to water before but maybe that will make all the difference," Brady said as he reached across the table for my hand.

* * *

After we left the restaurant we found a store that sold a charger for my phone. I plugged it into Brady's truck hoping it would work. I wasn't eager to call home, especially after our lunch conversation. The last thing I wanted to think about was home. I decided to send a quick text to my dad saying my phone was now working and that I would call him soon.

"So, Boston, eh? Why?" I asked.

"For the Red Sox of course," he joked. "But seriously, I looked at a lot of schools online and Boston appealed to me. After the last few days I've spent with you, it appeals to me even more." He grabbed my hand and kissed it.

I kept questioning in my mind what this was between us. I couldn't possibly be his girlfriend as we just met but here he was talking about Boston. I didn't want to get my hopes up too high. Boston would be perfect because there are a lot of opportunities for my field of work. Even if I stayed in Connecticut, Boston was only an hour away. I had to get off cloud nine and focus on the trip and this letter. Once I crossed that bridge, I could daydream about my fairy tale love story.

"Not much longer now," Brady said. "Why don't you try to take a nap and relax?"

I slid over next to him and laid my head on his shoulder. He kissed the top of my head and for the next hundred miles we didn't speak.

CHAPTER THIRTEEN

Brady gently shook me and said, "Anna, we're here." I opened up my eyes and saw that we were in a hotel parking lot. God, I hoped I didn't drool all over him. I pulled myself together, got out of the truck, and stretched my arms.

"Welcome to Portland," Brady said as he came over to the passenger's side and put his arms around me.

I looked around the parking lot and thought, *I made it.* I was finally in my grandmother's home town. Behind the hotel there were cornfields.

"What do you think?" asked Brady.

"We're not in Kansas anymore. Or are we?" I joked.

"Let's go check in and get some rest," Brady said. "Tomorrow will be a big day for you." He grabbed my bag and we walked into the lobby.

"Do you prefer two queens or a king room?" the clerk asked. Brady seemed nervous but replied, "Two queens will be just fine."

He handed us a key and we headed for the seventh floor. As we walked out of the elevator I realized that this would be the first time I had ever spent the night with a boy in a hotel room all alone. I thought about our previous conversation about the shower and had a burst of energy run through my body. I would never make a move though. Only in my mind was I an aggressive, forward girl. On the outside I was timid and reserved.

I hadn't had much experience with sex. I've only had one lover in my life and that was Carlo. I wasn't a prude or anything. I didn't see the point of making love without the love part. I had done *other* activities with boys that were not innocent but I definitely was no Chelsea.

Brady swiped the key card and opened the door for me. We both put our bags down and he came over to me and said, "Thank you again for allowing me to come on this trip with you."

As I smiled at him I could tell he was trying to get something out.

"About the two queen beds...I wanted you to feel comfortable with me. Of course, I would love to share a bed but you should get some rest tonight. If I were laying that close to you, I may have a hard time controlling myself."

"It's okay. I appreciate the gesture and you're right, we should both get a good night's sleep," I replied.

"I'm going to take a quick shower before going to bed." he said. Before he closed the bathroom door he flirtatiously whispered, "I'll leave the door open, ya know, just in case you want to join me."

I turned around and blushed like a pre-teen buying her first training bra. A huge part of me wanted to climb into the bed and hide under the covers. I opened the zipper of my bag and pulled out my boxer shorts and a tank top. I was disappointed with my PJ choice, not knowing I would have been in this situation. I guess that's why my mom always said it was important to prepare for anything. I probably should have listened to her.

I wondered if Brady really meant that I should join him in the shower. I hated how I could never read a guy's mind. I was more of a straight-to-the-point type of girl. If you want me, say so. Playing hard to get was fun but I had issues with rejection. The fact that he joked about leaving the door open made me unlock the bad girl inside of me. I was going to do it.

My heart began to pound. I was fearful that he would be able to hear me from inside the shower. I put one foot in front of the other and walked toward the bathroom door.

What in the world was I thinking? I barely know this guy. Those feelings did not seem to stop me as I slowly opened the bathroom door and let myself in. The sound of the water from the shower made me weak in the knees. I had a towel wrapped around my nude body. I could see his silhouette through the shower door. I thought about turning around and walking out.

Brady appeared through the door and softly said, "Anna, it's okay, I want you to come in with me." His hands took over my towel and I felt it drop to the floor. He had total control of my body. It was as if he held the remote to my every move. I climbed into the shower and felt the water soak my skin. Brady put shampoo in his hands and told me to turn around. He ran his fingers and his hands all through my hair. As he massaged my head I felt myself letting go. He led me back into the rain of the shower to rinse my hair. I then felt his fingertips crawl down my shoulders as he held me from behind. The way his body cupped mine felt erotic.

His lips kissed the back of my neck and I could feel his tongue taste my skin. He took my breath away. I turned around to see his face. I had never seen anything more beautiful than the way the water dripped over his olive-toned skin. His wet, wavy hair curled more in the shower and a strand fell into his face. *I must be dreaming*. Without saying a word, his lips kissed mine and we began a long, passionate make out session right there under the showerhead. It was straight out of a soft porn movie, yet tasteful. Hands were roaming and mouths were exploring. I had never had this kind of foreplay before. I liked it.

Brady was such a gentleman. He would ask me if I was okay. He told me he would stop if I wasn't comfortable. I never thought taking a shower with a man could be so intimate. Chelsea told me once that foreplay can sometimes be more intimate than the actual act of sex. I could only imagine what the sex would be like. We stepped out of the shower, dried off our bodies, and climbed into bed, barely making it to "third base." There were no home run hits but it left me wanting more.

"Should I stay here or do you want me to go sleep over there?" I asked as I pointed to the other queen bed that was still nicely made.

"Close your eyes and dream with me," he whispered as he slowly passed out.

My heart jumped out of my skin when I heard a big boom. As I opened my eyes, I could see lightening beaming through the curtains. Once I realized it was just a storm my heart returned to its normal pace.

As I laid there in Brady's arms I stared at the wall. I couldn't fall back to sleep so my mind just wandered. I thought about my dad and how he was handling my mom and me both being gone. I wondered how my grandfather was doing, having been pulled in every direction. He must miss grandma a lot.

With Brady's arms wrapped around me, I thought about how my poor grandpa had a spot missing in his own bed where his love used to sleep. I felt safe and secure being next to someone. It was all new to me but routine to my grandpa. Now, while I'm here getting used to the comfort of someone else, he is getting used to an empty bed. A tear slowly streamed down my face. *Would that be me someday? Would I be lying in an empty bed missing the love of my life?*

I noticed a Bible on the night table. I was done thinking about Heaven and religion lately and no matter how hard I tried, I couldn't stop. My faith had been questioned. It pained me to think that death was the end. Is that why people created religion? To make dying easier, or was there truth to God and Heaven? When I talked to friends about it, they would tell me, "It's better to have faith, so they just believe."

I even asked a priest back home and he told me I was completely normal. He said that most people who experience the death of a loved one either feel closer to God or further away. I asked him how I get back to my faith in God. After all, my grandmother went to church every Sunday and believed. Unfortunately, faith isn't something you can teach. You have to feel it. It bothered me that I wasn't feeling it anymore.

The thunder must have also startled Brady because he had woken up and noticed I was awake.

"Are you okay?" he whispered.

I grabbed a hold of his hand that was around me and kissed it. "Never felt safer."

He held me tight as his eyes closed and he went back to sleep. I knew it would be a big day for me so I had to try to fall asleep myself. It's always hard to sleep when you know the following day is going to be something important, like the first day of school. You know you need to rest for the big day, yet your mind won't let you relax enough.

I felt Brady's fingertips tickle my arm. My mother used to do this to put me to sleep. *How did he know I couldn't sleep and this was the trick?* Before I could keep thinking, I was out like a light.

* * *

We set no alarms and didn't utilize any wake-up calls. We just slept. As I was enjoying this relaxing moment, my phone went off.

"What's that?" Brady asked as he rolled over onto his back.

I climbed out of bed and said, "It's just my phone. Someone sent me a text message."

"What time is it?" he asked.

I looked at my phone and saw that it was almost 10:00 a.m. "Wow, it's just about ten o'clock."

"I can't remember the last time I slept in," Brady said.

"I know. Me neither." I said as I climbed back up into the bed. I looked down at my phone. "It's my friend Chelsea checking on me."

"It's nice to have friends who care," he said with a big yawn.

"Yeah, she's great."

"You will have a lot to tell her when you get back home, huh?"

"I'm hoping I will be able to show and tell," I said with a laugh.

"Oh, you were one of those kids in school who liked show and tell."

I leaned closer to him and said, "Well, when you have something great to share, yes."

He sat up next to me and kissed my forehead. "I'm going to get ready, so why don't you call your father now?" he suggested.

"I know, I should." As he closed the bathroom door and turned the shower on, I dialed home.

"Anna, I am so glad to hear your voice and am relieved your cell phone is fixed," my dad said.

"I found a mall area so I'm all set, Dad. I just wanted to let you know I'm doing well."

"Glad to hear it, sweetheart. I wish I could stay and talk to you, but I'm running late for a meeting at work. I am literally outside the door."

"Dad, it's okay. I will call you again but wanted you to know I am headed for Chicago to see some sights then will come home," I blurted out quick.

"Chicago? Just please be careful. Chicago is a rough city. No walking those city streets at night."

"I know, Dad. I will be careful, I promise," I said as I tried to reassure him.

"Love you, Anna," he said as he hung up the phone.

Brady walked out of the bathroom wearing jeans and a white button-down shirt. His sleeves were rolled up and he looked yummy. I didn't want to leave the room. His hair was still wet as he pushed gel into it with his fingers. The gel must have been scented or he put on cologne because he smelled divine.

"Everything okay on the home front?" he asked.

"Everything is just fine," I said.

"I guess I should go get ready myself." Brady stole a kiss on my cheek as I walked by him toward the bathroom. Sometimes I wondered if he did certain things because he knew how lustful it would make me feel. I am not the same girl I was when I left Connecticut. My hormones are out of control.

"There's a cool-looking coffee shop about three blocks from the hotel. I was thinking we could stop there for breakfast while we figure out the plan," he said.

I popped my head out of the bathroom and said, "Sounds perfect."

As we left the hotel and walked outside, I closed my eyes and took a deep breath. I made it. If Brady had never stopped for me, who knows where I would be at this moment. Maybe I'd still be sitting there on the side of the road. I glanced over at him as he was looking around the area. Somehow it felt like we rescued each other. Even if it didn't end up in marriage, I had a feeling we would forever be a part of each other's lives.

Portland was a cute little town. It was clean, and the buildings were sculpted with beautiful architecture. Main Street was especially nice to look at. Although the buildings were dated, they were well kept. After driving through mostly flat farmlands, Portland was like a hidden gem. I wondered if any of these businesses were around when my grandmother had lived here. Brady took my hand as we crossed the road to the coffee shop. It was a little cozy place right on the corner.

"What a cute place!" I said.

"Coffee Cup Cafe, how original," Brady replied as he held the door open for me.

We grabbed a small table nestled by the window so we could people-watch.

"What would you like?" Brady asked.

"I guess I'll have an iced French Vanilla and a croissant."

"No Mocha with whipped cream this time?" he asked jokingly as he walked over to get our breakfast. As he put down the food and coffees I tried to give him some money but again he refused. "I appreciate you trying to pay Anna, but I have plenty to share and I want to spend it on you. I tell you what, if I run out, I will let you know, okay?"

I shyly thanked him. I wasn't used to having someone take care of me outside my family.

"So what do you want to do first?" he asked.

I thought for a moment and said, "I'd like to find the house my grandmother grew up in."

"That's cool. Do you know the street name?"

"Yeah, I am pretty sure it's called Moody Avenue. I found that information through some genealogy website."

Brady pulled out his phone from his pocket. "Let's see if my navigation can get us to Moody Avenue," he said. "It looks to be about twelve blocks from here and a couple of small turns. After we're done eating we can go back to the hotel and grab the truck."

"I feel like I can't say it enough, but I truly appreciate everything you have and continue to do for me," I replied as I put my hand over his.

"Anna, I am happy seeing you happy."

How would I ever be able to repay him for his kindness?

* * *

We got back in his truck at the hotel and began the first part of our journey. I was amazed at all the current restaurants and stores they had in Portland. When I first imagined what Indiana would be like, I thought of mostly farms. Although they had all the up-to-date amenities, I still saw a few horse-drawn carriages on the main roads.

"I think this is it," Brady said as he put his blinker on to make a left.

He was right. It was Moody Avenue. I peered out the window at all the old houses. One of these homes was where she lived. I just had no idea which one it was. These homes looked as if they were built in the early 1900s, so I was sure she lived in one of them. As I viewed each one, I imagined what it was like back when Grandma lived here. I thought about her father pulling in the driveway and her running out the front door to greet him. She had always spoken of her dad and how much she missed him. She would tell me stories about her childhood but would often cry.

When her father passed away, her mother moved her to Connecticut. She never recalled a funeral for him and it seemed like they were rushed out of state. Her mother told her it was to help ease the pain and to make a new start. My grandmother thought it was because her father's parents were trying to get custody of her and her brother. She explained how her mother wasn't the most responsible woman back then. Her mother chose Connecticut because it's where her sister Fiona was living.

When she came to Connecticut, her mother fell in love with a new man and they married a year after her father's death. My grandmother hated her stepfather. He was horrible to her and made her quit school in the eighth grade to get a job. She often wondered if her life would have been better if she had stayed in Indiana. My grandmother would then smile and say, "But if I didn't come to Connecticut, I wouldn't have my life with Poppy."

Her mother ended up having two more children with the new husband. My grandmother helped raise them. She loved her younger brother and sister but had really lost her childhood at that point. I think that is why she loved being around kids. My grandmother always had her heart set on going back to Indiana. I wanted to take her so badly but her illness got in the way and then it was too late. It taught me a valuable lesson. All we ever have is the present.

"Do you want me to pull over so we can walk down the street?" Brady asked.

"Sure," I replied as I woke up from my daydreaming.

We parked the car on the side of the road and got out. The breeze was perfect on this sunny day. Moody Avenue wasn't a big street. There were only about six houses on the entire road. I wondered if my grandmother had walked in the exact spots my steps were taking. I heard a couple of birds singing nearby in a tree. When I looked over, I noticed a tire swing hanging off the branch.

Could this be the house? My grandmother used to tell me about a tire swing she would swing on in her front yard while she waited for her father to come home.

"I think this is it," I said to Brady.

He looked at my face and then at the house. "You think this is the one she lived in? How can you tell?" he asked.

"Because she used to tell me stories about the tire swing hanging in the tree in her front yard. This is the only house on this street with a tire swing in the front yard," I said.

"This is great, Anna. Let's go check it out," he said.

"Wait!" I said as I grabbed his arm. "We can't just go into someone's yard."

"Why not? You New England people are a little tense. I'm sure this family won't mind. Look, there's the homeowner now watering the garden. Let's go talk to her," he said as he took hold of my hand.

The woman looked to be in her mid-forties. When she saw us approaching her, she stopped. To my surprise, she had a welcoming smile on her face. "Can I help you with something?" she asked.

Brady spoke to her as I was too nervous. "Yes, ma'am. My girlfriend believes that this house may have been the home her grandmother lived in as a child. Was that tire swing here when you moved into this home?"

"Oh yes, it sure was. This was my parent's home. They bought it in 1941 and when my mom passed away ten years ago, I decided to move in with my family. I also grew up here and used that tire swing pretty much every day. I still do sometimes," she said with a big smile.

"I'm Anna," I said to her as I reached out to shake her hand.

"Anna, it's a pleasure to meet you. My name is Jillian Croft. So you think your grandmother lived in this house?"

"Yes, I do, and it was 1941 when she moved to Connecticut, so I really feel like this is the house."

Mrs. Croft's phone started to ring inside her home. "Would you please excuse me? I better go get that. Please feel free to walk around the property. I surely don't mind one bit," she said as she walked toward the house.

"She seems like a real nice lady," Brady said as we walked toward the tire swing. "Why don't you give it a try?"

"I don't know. This is someone else's home…"

He guided me over to the swing and said, "Sit on it. I'm pretty sure Jillian doesn't mind."

I sat on the tire swing and Brady gave me a push. I glanced up at the tree and all the leaves. It was a huge oak tree and it was sturdy and strong. It must have been to withstand the tire swing all these years.

As Brady kept pushing me higher and higher, I felt like a child again. I felt peaceful and calm. It must have been why my grandmother loved this swing so much. Brady took out his phone and snapped a picture of me on the swing. He then slowed me down and hugged me from behind on the swing and took a picture of both of us.

"I want this to be our first picture together," he said. "This moment means so much to you and now I am forever a part of it." A teardrop fell from my eyes. He wiped it off my cheek and our lips met for a kiss.

Jillian had made her way outside again and was carrying a couple of glasses in her hand. She walked over to us and said, "Would you folks like a cup of iced tea?" We took the glasses and thanked her for her hospitality.

"Thank you, Mrs. Croft, for giving me this moment. My grandmother always talked about her childhood and this swing. I can see why she liked it and why your family does too," I said as I took a sip of the tea.

"You are so welcome, Anna. It's nice to meet a piece of history here today. Your grandmother sounds like she was someone special to you."

"She was like my second mother. I came here for her," I replied.

"You know she is with you? We mothers never leave our children's sides, even long after we're gone. My mom is with me every day, especially when I'm in the garden. It's something we liked to do together," she explained.

"Thank you for sharing that. I really hope she is with me," I said as I handed her my empty glass.

"All you need is a little faith so you hang onto whatever memories you have of her and never let them go," said Jillian.

"I sure won't. I'm glad we decided to get out of the car and take this walk," I said.

"I'm glad too. You two make a lovely couple and I wish you both all the best. Enjoy the rest of your visit."

"We will, and thanks again for the tea," Brady said as he took my hand and we walked back to the truck.

"Wow, she was really nice," I said.

"See, it wasn't so bad."

"If we were in Connecticut, the owners probably would have called the police because we were on their property," I replied.

Brady shook his head and said, "That's sad because there are good people left in this world."

"I am learning that as I continue on with this adventure," I said.

"Where is our next adventure?" Brady asked with intrigue.

"The cemetery," I replied. We pulled out onto the main road and I started to feel somber.

"You okay, Anna?" Brady asked.

"Yes, I'm just taking it all in."

"This can't be an easy thing to do. We don't have to go to the cemetery right now if you don't want to." Trying to cheer me up, he added, "We can go get drunk someplace."

I laughed and said, "I may need to get drunk later so perhaps we should save that for the nighttime. And I am a very fun drunk, I might add," I flirtatiously said.

"There's that smile back. Do you have any idea where the cemetery may be located?" he asked.

"Not a clue."

"I'm going to drive back to the hotel and we can talk to the concierge desk. They should be able to help us out," he said.

To our surprise, there was no concierge desk. We were hopeful that someone at the front desk could help us find Center Cemetery. We tried to look online and use navigation systems on our phones but nothing came up. The girl behind the desk had no idea but she was going to get a manager who has lived in the area all her life to help. About five minutes later, a petite, older woman showed up who knew exactly where the cemetery was.

"It's the oldest cemetery in Jay County. It's not that easy to find but if you follow these directions, you should run right into it," she said as she showed us a map. "You will think you are driving out to the middle of nowhere because that is exactly where Center Cemetery is. I only know this because my mother-in-law lives out that way. Here, take this map in case you need it." She folded the map and handed it to us.

"Thank you so much for your help," I replied. We hopped back into his truck once again and headed for nowhere.

* * *

"I guess that woman was right. It's like we left all civilization," Brady said.

There were huge farms, much larger than any I've ever seen. The scenery was quite astonishing. There were a few beautiful ranch homes set on about twenty acres of farmland. I almost felt like it could be a place I would want to live. To have all that peace and quiet would be divine. I wondered if the people who lived out here survived longer because the stress levels were lower. Then again, it was a lot of land to work. I would need plenty of money to pay people to do it for me.

"It's charming out here. Something about it makes me feel calm and rested," I said to Brady.

"Probably be a nice place to retire but I don't know if I would want all the responsibility to care for that much land," he said.

He read my mind about the land. "True, but that's why you hire help to do it for you," I said with a smile.

"Now you're talking," Brady said. "Any idea where his grave is located in the cemetery?"

"Not a clue," I replied.

"So you are hoping to just get lucky?"

"I am always hoping for that," I said as I started to blush.

"You're addicting," he said, so seriously.

Me? Addicting? He really must never venture out of Yellow Springs. I started to feel a little fearful. *What if all this romance goes away the more he gets to know me?* Life surely was easier being single. Perhaps I *was* still single. We haven't known each other long enough to be going steady. He did refer to me as his *girlfriend* to that woman, Jillian, on Moody Avenue, however. I had to stop thinking so much.

"Anna, did I say something wrong?" he asked.

He probably thought he did because after that amazing compliment, I said nothing, not even a simple *thank you.* "Not at all. In fact, you've said everything right since the moment we met," I said. I took a deep breath and blurted out, "I'm just scared."

Brady abruptly pulled the truck off to the side of the road. He looked at me with this stare and it felt like he had taken over my entire being. He turned the ignition off and scooted closer to me.

Before I could say a word, he grabbed hold of my waist, pulled me into him, and kissed me like he was never going to see me again. It was so passionate that he now had me lying down on the seat as he crawled on top of me. His hands wandered over my body as his lips kissed my neck, my chest, and any other area he could easily get to without ripping my clothes off. He pulled my shirt off over my head. When I felt his lips around my belly button and his tongue playfully kiss me, I melted.

Were we going to do it right here and now in his truck? I wanted to, badly. I could still smell the scent of his hair gel and I remembered how hot he looked coming out of the bathroom this morning. I roamed his chiseled body with my hands and kissed whatever parts of his body I could reach. Brady was so spontaneous and he made me feel helpless in his arms. All I could think of was, *Forgive me father, for I want to sin.*

A huge farm-type truck drove by and startled us. It didn't help that he honked his horn as he drove by. It seemed like he was giving Brady a high-five. He deserved it though. Brady sat up in his seat and was panting and laughing at how we got caught out.

"How do you feel now?" he asked.

I looked over at him as I was sitting there in just my bra and jeans and said, "Honestly, I'm horny."

"Yeah, I am too. Mission accomplished," he said as he started up the truck again.

I didn't quite know what he meant by that. "Mission accomplished?" I asked curiously.

"Yes, you told me you were scared. I don't want you to feel that way so I'd rather have you feeling horny than scared, therefore, mission accomplished."

As I pulled my shirt back on over my bare skin, I whispered in his ear, "I think you may have more of a mission to fulfill later."

He took a deep breath like he was trying to control the emotions gearing toward sex and said, "That won't be a problem," and he pulled back onto the road.

"I think this is it," he said as we arrived at the cemetery. The sign read "Center Cemetery," and there was a cute little white church on the property. "Well, it shouldn't be too difficult to find the stones because there aren't that many here," Brady said.

He was right. There were probably no more than a hundred people buried here.

"Do you want me to go with you and look or do you want to go alone?" he asked.

"I'd like you to come," I said and we both got out of the truck. "What a cute church," I said.

"I bet it's really old and cool inside," he said. Brady walked over to see if the church was opened. As he tried to open the doors, he noticed it was locked. "It looks like they still have services here because the times are posted and the paint is pretty new."

I started looking at some of the stones. Brady came over to join me. "What name are we looking for?" he asked.

"Schroll."

"I'll go look over here and see what I can find," he said.

"Thanks."

I looked at all the stones and wondered what kind of life these people had. Did anyone in my family know them? It was a small town after all.

Rows and rows of stones, yet I didn't come across any Schroll's. I started to feel discouraged. I remember my grandmother saying she bought a stone for her father, Roy, because she didn't think he had one. She said she bought it and had it shipped to Indiana. That was one of the reasons she wanted to return. She wanted to put flowers on his grave.

"I think I found it," Brady called out.

I walked over to where he was standing. Sure enough, the stone read "Schroll." I stared down at it and was a little confused. Her father's name was Royal Earl so I expected to see a stone that said Roy or Earl but all that was there was Clara and John.

"This is the stone for my grandmother's father's parents," I said as I sat wondering where Roy's was.

"Maybe he is buried with them because he couldn't afford a stone," said Brady.

"But I remember my grandmother telling me that she had bought a stone for him," I explained.

"Did she say it was specifically for him or could it be for his family?" Brady asked.

Now I was all confused. "I'm pretty sure she said she got a stone for her father."

"Maybe they're not buried in the same spot. Let's keep looking," Brady replied.

We looked up and down every single aisle and even looked twice. There was no sign of Royal Earl Schroll anywhere. I felt stuck because now that my grandmother was gone, how would I ever know if she bought the stone that said John and Clara or if the stone for her father was somewhere else? Brady came over and noticed my frustration.

"I'm sorry, Anna. Hey, maybe that cousin of yours will know more about it," he said with some enthusiasm.

I wasn't sure how much this cousin would know because my grandmother didn't even know who she was. Although, she was a relative on her father's side so perhaps she had some answers for me. I walked back over to John and Clara's stone and sat for a moment. Brady went back into his truck to give me a few minutes alone. I felt like I had to talk to them. I wanted them to know just how much my grandmother missed their son all those years.

"Well, I'm here. My grandmother always spoke of Indiana and her father. I took this trip for her. I hope she is up in Heaven with you guys. Please let her know I miss her every day and I will never forget to think about her," I said, talking to the stone.

I began to cry. Here I was in this peaceful cemetery on the most beautiful day I've seen all year, with temps in the mid 70s, a nice breeze, and the sun shining. I looked around the cemetery and at the corn fields. The wind was gently blowing them and I thought, *What a beautiful place to rest!* I closed my eyes and felt the breeze on my face. Maybe my grandmother was home, back in Indiana where her heart was. She used to say how much she loved her childhood here. It was at this moment that I knew why. As I wiped my tears and got to my feet, I knew I would never forget the way I felt right now. My heavy shoulders were now lighter. This moment made my extreme trip out here worth it.

I opened the passenger side door and climbed into the truck. As we pulled away from the cemetery I looked back at it with joy. It was a magical place full of love and peace. A part of me stayed there that day and I may never get it back.

CHAPTER FOURTEEN

"It's almost five-thirty," Brady said. "How about we grab some dinner?"

"Sounds great, I'm pretty hungry." I moved closer to him and put my head on his shoulder. That was the best thing about a pick-up truck. You could still sit next to the driver.

We stopped at a cute little restaurant called The Palmer House. It was old-fashioned and endearing. The restaurant looked like an old wealthy home you would find on a main street back in the day. It was made of bricks and had pillars in the front.

When you first walked in, there was a small library they turned into the waiting area. What a great idea to make the waiting area relaxing for the customers. A few were sitting by the fireplace, reading. On the other side of the library/waiting area, there was a small bar. The wood looked old and classic. The whole restaurant was lit by either the lamps that hung on the wall or lanterns on each table. Most of the patrons were older so I think we stumbled upon fine dining.

"Do you think this place it too expensive?" I asked Brady.

"This place is cool. We are definitely going to eat here, regardless of cost. I hope it is expensive because then I can finally take you out on a proper date," he replied as he squeezed my hand.

The waitress came over and sat us at a table that looked as if it were made for royalty. The chairs were antique and they even had a "man" chair and a "lady" chair. The man chair had arms while the lady chair was without. It seemed a little sexist but I couldn't take my eyes off of the décor.

"I love the wood beams," I said to Brady.

"Yeah, me too. I like how everything is old and rustic," he said as his eyes looked around the restaurant.

"Are you ready to order?" asked the elegant-looking waitress.

"We are," said Brady. "She will have the filet mignon, medium rare, with the vegetables and a baked potato. I will have the baked stuffed shrimp and a crock of onion soup. We will also take a bottle of the Mondavi Merlot." He ordered so elegantly.

"Very well," she said as she walked away.

"You sounded so graceful and poised," I smiled over at Brady.

"I'm glad because I am trying really hard to impress you."

"Every time you open your mouth, touch my hand, or kiss my lips, you impress me," I replied.

"If I wasn't trapped in this manly chair, I would come over there and kiss you now," he said.

"You can make up for it later," I said as I took a sip of my water.

This was a high-class place. We had three different waiters and people cleaning up our table. They even brought us sorbet between the salad dish and the main course. As they put the sorbet down in front of us, they told us it was to cleanse our palette. I was afraid to see the bill since it was all à la carte.

"How's your shrimp?" I asked Brady.

"It will be well worth the money," he said. "Are you enjoying that filet?"

"It's almost gone so that should be a telltale sign," I replied as I took a sip of the wine.

"I'm glad you like it. Make sure you save room for dessert."

"I plan on having dessert but not here." The wine was most definitely influencing my words but I liked it. The truth was I wanted this boy.

After spending all of Brady's life savings at the restaurant, we headed back to the hotel.

* * *

"Are you nervous about tomorrow?" Brady asked.

"Very," I replied.

"It will be okay. So far, everything has worked out."

I loved how he consoled me. Most guys wouldn't care to ask because they don't like to get involved in deep conversations. Not Brady, he surely was different.

When we got back to the room, Brady's cell phone was ringing. Since he was in the bathroom, he yelled out to me to answer his phone. I think he thought it would be his mother. When I said hello, I received a whole other surprise.

"Who is this?" a woman said in an overly forward voice.

"Anna," I simply responded.

"Well, Anna, this is Danielle. Brady's mother told me he took off with some girl to Indiana. I just wanted to let you know that he is mine."

Caught off-guard, I answered, "Brady has never mentioned you to me but maybe you should speak with him."

"I'm sure he didn't mention the fact that I was pregnant with his baby either?" she explained.

My heart was failing. I could feel the disappointment and shock come over my body. I wanted to hang up the phone and run out of the hotel room. *A baby?* He has been playing this nice boy act with me and now I felt like a fool.

"He didn't tell me about the baby. I'll make sure he calls you," I said as I hung up the phone and set it down on the table.

Brady came out of the bathroom wrapped in a towel and asked who it was. I couldn't find the words to speak so I said nothing. I grabbed my purse and said, "I need to get some air."

I walked out of the hotel and made my way down the street. I sat on a bench that was outside a little garden area. It was completely dark except for the few lampposts. The road was quiet. I sat there and stared into the blank air. *How could this happen? I should have known he was too good to be true.* I wasn't sure how I would ever finish this trip now. He was the last person in the world I wanted to see.

I heard Brady calling my name. I didn't want to answer him and was upset he found me. At that moment, I wanted to be alone.

"Anna, there is so much to explain," he said.

I looked up at him and said, "No, not really, Brady. I think I got the story from Danielle."

He sat down next to me on the bench and leaned in to talk with me. "I am not dating Danielle. I was never in love with her. We all have a past, Anna."

"Yes, we do, but not all of us have babies with someone and run off with some stranger," I replied as I felt my heart bang through my chest.

"You're not some stranger. I'm in love with you, Anna." His fingers moved my hair out of my face and behind my ear. "I had a fling. It was a drunken few weeks with the wrong girl. We did the deed and I used protection. She tried telling me she was pregnant. This was after I explained to her as gently as possible that I didn't feel for her that way. Ever since then, she throws around this pregnancy thing. She is hurting and thinks it will change my mind."

"How do you know she isn't pregnant?" I asked as a tear streamed down my cheek.

"It's a small town and my friend's sister is the OBGYN. When she saw Danielle, she told her she wasn't pregnant. Danielle has had a rough life and she desperately wants someone to love her. It's just not me."

"This is again why I'm scared. We barely know each other and after all this is over, I just don't know what's going to happen. This trip has been fun and I like to think of us as more than just a fling, but you have a life in Ohio," I said.

"I can't tell you that what we have is forever, but I can tell you that I'd like to see where it can go. We do know each other, Anna. I've never felt like this before and please don't let one phone call ruin it. If it would make you feel better, I will call my friend's sister and have her tell you about Danielle and how she is not pregnant, and that we are not dating."

As I sat there and listened to Brady explain his case, I realized nothing is perfect. He was involved with a girl and they had a pregnancy scare. It doesn't make him a bad person nor should I be sitting here judging him. He has been amazing since I met him, so why would I let some girl ruin it.

"Can you come to me, please?" he asked with the most sincere look in his eyes. I moved in closer as he held me tight.

We sat on the bench and cuddled. It was getting chilly but I felt warm. He stroked my hair and kissed my cheek. I didn't like how we sort of had our first fight. For some reason I wanted to cry. I thought about all the sadness in my life. Before I could lose a tear, he started talking again.

"I am serious about Boston University. After meeting you, I am more confident that it's where I want to go. You make me want to be a better person. I can't promise what the next five years or five days will be like. I can promise you that I will do my best to get to know every part of you, the good, the bad, and all that stands in between."

Yet again, he has consoled me. All I could say was, "I want to take you back to the room."

* * *

As the door of our hotel room closed, my mood changed. I didn't care about Danielle or her issues. Even if Brady was telling me lies, tonight I didn't care. I was going to make love to him. If he was all talk, he was good. "I'm going to run a quick bath if you don't mind?" I said to Brady. I figured it would be a great way to relax after what happened tonight and to prepare for tomorrow.

"I don't mind at all. I'll be right here waiting for you," he said as he climbed into bed and turned on the television.

I decided to take the letter in with me from my grandmother's cousin. The jets in the tub were glorious. I could easily fall asleep. As I read the letter again from Freda, I prayed the news she had for my grandmother would be good. She didn't mention any clues in her words, only that she needed to speak to her about information regarding the family. Either way, I had to finish this journey, no matter what the outcome. I put the letter back into the envelope and made my way out to Brady. He surely would take my mind off the anxiety.

I walked out of the bathroom wrapped in a towel. Brady was standing by the window. He walked toward me and reached out for my waist. I felt vulnerable but in a good way. His warm hands took the towel and threw it onto the floor. I was completely nude standing before him.

"You're so beautiful," he whispered in my ear.

It began. Every inch of me was tingling. I lusted after his every touch, his every kiss. His hands ran through my hair as he kissed my lips. It wasn't his normal soft kisses but a deeper, more exotic kiss. He wasn't sloppy, but he was forceful, and I have to admit I liked it.

His fingertips teased my nipples. He gave my body a rise. My breathing became heavy as he touched areas that normally are covered up and hidden. He took his time and moved me slowly over to the bed. He laid me down and just stared for a moment. It was like I belonged to him. He owned me. His eyes seduced me, his hands discovered me, and his lips tasted me.

"I want to kiss you so that when we're apart, every single inch of you misses me," he said in the most sensual voice.

He climbed over me and put my hands over my head, holding me down. The only thing I could do was let him have me. I looked up at the ceiling as I could feel him ascend up between my legs. His lips made their way up my thighs. My toes began to curl and I couldn't catch my breath.

I don't even remember if I'd ever had a real orgasm. Brady felt sinful and delicious. The way his lips sweet-talked my womanhood was so erotic. I grabbed hold of his hair and he knew I was close to budding. When he came back up and looked me in the eyes, he crossed into my threshold.

While we made love, a little more than strangers, his kisses were stupefying. I loved his lips and the way they fit in mine so perfectly. It was almost like playing Tetris but every part that met was harmonious. I had never been kissed this way before. We were one. The night couldn't have been more perfect if it came straight out of a novel.

"I could get used to this," I whispered in his ear.

"I don't want you to get used to anything. It should always be spontaneous," he replied as he kissed my forehead and laid down next to me.

CHAPTER FIFTEEN

I set the alarm for nine o'clock. I crawled out of bed and looked over at Brady. He was still sleeping. I smiled as I reminisced about last night. I knew why Chelsea liked sex so much. I wondered if she had ever experienced a man like Brady before. I couldn't wait to tell her *some* of the details.

I jumped into the shower. As I was washing my hair I heard Brady's cell phone ring. A part of me was worried it was Danielle again. I hated that feeling of jealousy. The good thing about being single for so long was that I didn't have to deal with that.

I turned the water off and stepped out of the tub. As I dried my hair with the towel, I could tell he was talking with his mother. I have to admit it made me feel better knowing it was her and not Danielle. Even though I was angry at this girl, I understood Brady's points about her. He sort of protected her dignity but also comforted me. I had a feeling he learned a lot of his respect for people from his mother.

I walked out of the bathroom and found Brady already dressed in his jeans and a polo shirt. For a Midwestern cowboy, he dressed very GQ. When he was working, he played the part of a rugged cowboy but outside of work he was more "business casual." I liked every look on him. It would make for a great sex life.

Sex! Why was I constantly thinking about sex? It must be because Brady was like sex on a stick.

As I dabbed on some of my perfume, Brady came up behind me and said, "You smell Heavenly."

"It's how you make me feel," I said as I leaned back and kissed his cheek.

"Did you want to grab breakfast at that coffee shop again?" Brady asked.

"I think I'd rather have a quick cup of coffee here and then head to Dunkirk if that's okay?"

"Sounds good," he replied as he pulled my hair back away from my face.

We made our way down to the lobby and filled our coffee cups. They also had a few pastries on a plate. Brady and I helped ourselves to a muffin before walking out to the truck. My stomach was feeling rather upset. I know it was from my nerves and probably the coffee. Luckily, I had a Pepto-Bismol tablet in my purse so I took two, hoping it would relax me and prevent any tummy issues.

"Thank you for last night. I hope it wasn't too soon for you?" he said.

"I wanted to. I've wanted to since the moment you rescued me."

"It was really good, just so you know," he said with his flirty smile. "Best I've had."

I started to feel my face getting red. *Do I tell him I thought it was good too? I didn't have much to compare it to but I thought it was amazing.*

"I haven't had many lovers," I said to him. *Oh my god, why did I just say that?*

"So not much to compare me to then, eh?" he said a little disappointed.

"No, no, I don't need anyone to use as a comparison. Last night was beyond amazing. It was like those moments when you can't find the right words," I replied.

He smiled and said, "Well, sometimes the most beautiful things in the world can't be seen with the eyes. They must be felt with the heart. I sound corny. I'm sorry, Anna."

"Please don't apologize. You make me feel things I never have before. I'm jumping out of my skin because I don't know how to control it. I'm the girl who never takes chances," I explained.

Brady looked in my eyes and said, "I'm glad you took this chance, this trip. I don't want to disappoint you or make you scared. I feel those things too. At the same time, that's life. I think we need to enjoy what we have now and worry about the future when we need to, okay?"

"Okay," I agreed.

"Now, let's get you to Dunkirk so you can take some more chances."

As we drove a few more miles up the road, I started to see signs for Dunkirk. I tried not to get nervous but it was hard. I had that feeling you get before you go on stage to do a speech or it's your turn to bat and there are two "outs" and the whole game depends on you. I put my hands together and quietly prayed to my grandmother that she would help me get through this day. A glare from the sun came through the window and I felt her with me.

"What's the address for your cousin?" Brady asked.

I pulled out the letter and said, "Eight-twenty-one South Main Street." He plugged it into the GPS and we were on our way. Every time the English woman spoke the directions, I felt a tornado in my stomach. I knew we were getting close.

"This is South Main Street," Brady said. The houses all looked like The Palmer House restaurant. It was an older town with all these huge colonials lined up along the road. Some of them even had widow watchtowers. "There it is," Brady pointed as he pulled alongside the curb across the street.

It was the perfect country house with a big old wraparound porch. The siding was white with black shutters. The landscaping was beautiful and professionally manicured. There was even a gazebo set up in the back yard. At that moment, I was glad I wore my sundress. These relatives of mine certainly had some money.

"Are you ready to go in?" Brady asked. "Do you want me to stay here in the truck?"

"I think I'd feel better if you came. I fear I may pass out or something, if you don't mind?" I asked.

"Not at all, come on," he said as we got out of the truck.

With every step up the walkway I felt more nervous. I hoped I wouldn't trip over my own feet. We stood on the doorstep and Brady knew I wouldn't have the nerve to ring the bell so he leaned over and rang it for me. I wanted to run as fast as I could away from that door. *What in the world was I doing here?* My family was going to kill me when they found out what I've done. *But what about what they've done?*

It didn't matter now because the door had just opened and a woman who looked like Kathy Bates was standing there looking at Brady and me.

"Can I help you?" she asked, looking like we were trying to sell her something.

I froze but I knew I had to thaw out quickly. "My name is Anna Corolla and this is my friend Brady. Are you by chance Freda Anderson?"

"I am. What can I do for you?" she asked.

"I found this letter you wrote to my grandmother," I said as I handed her the envelope.

She looked down at it for a moment and then looked back up at me. "Well, come on in," she said as she opened the door for us. "Why don't you both have a seat there in the living room and I will get us some lemonade."

"See, it's all going to be okay," Brady said as he took my hand and we sat down on the couch.

The living room had nautical décor and was elegantly decorated. I felt like we were in a Martha Stewart Home magazine. Everything was perfect in its place. Freda walked back into the room with glasses filled with lemonade and a plate of cookies.

"I actually just baked these this morning," she said as she put them down on the coffee table. "I make my special peanut butter cookies for the town fair every year. It's happening this weekend. Have you two ever been?" she asked.

I replied and said, "No, I live in Connecticut and Brady is from Ohio."

"Oh I see. Did your grandmother send you here to find out about my letter? It has been over two years since I sent that," Freda explained.

"No, she didn't send me. In fact, if she were able, she would have been the one to come and talk to you. My grandmother passed away a few months back," I said a bit choked up.

"Oh dear, I'm awfully sorry to hear this."

Freda looked a bit distraught over the news, as if she had known my grandmother. She looked down at her lap and seemed disappointed. Whatever that letter entailed must be something important.

"I was doing my thesis paper over my grandparent's house and I accidently came across your unopened letter. I'm guessing that she misplaced it and never had the chance to read it. Normally my grandmother was really good at that kind of thing so I was surprised myself to find it," I explained.

"So your family sent you to come and see me?" Freda questioned.

"Not exactly. They don't know I came here. They think I'm traveling to Chicago to go sightseeing on a college graduation road trip."

Freda looked a bit confused. "Why didn't you want to tell them?"

I took a deep breath and explained what I could to her. "My family has turned into complete drama since the passing of my grandmother. My aunts are fighting over my grandmother's will. My mom checked herself into rehab for drinking, leaving my father home to mourn on his own. I needed the escape. I couldn't take their arguing anymore. My grandmother dies and they fall apart."

Freda sat there for a moment and took in what I just told her.

"Anna, I'm deeply sorry to hear about what is going on with your family. It is also a blessing that you have come to see me. I still can't believe you hopped in your car alone and drove all this way, but I'm glad you did. I have a feeling that by the time you leave here, you will also feel like this trip was a blessing," she said.

Her words comforted me and I felt more confident that the news must be something good.

"I am your grandmother's cousin on her father's side, as you now know. My mother was Royal Earl's sister. After my mom passed away, I grew fond of genealogy and wanted to learn more about my heritage. That is where this letter comes in to play. I learned something that changed my life and it most definitely will change your family's as well. In fact, I hope that when you return home, all the family issues are diminished," she explained.

"I hope so too," I replied.

She got up and went over to a table with a wooden box sitting on it. She picked it up and brought it over to the coffee table in front of us. "This is the box that has all my research in it. There are pictures of relatives, family tree information, obituaries, and marriage and death certificates inside. Feel free to take a look," she said.

As I looked through some of the things in that box, I said, "Wow, looks like you did a lot of work."

"Well, what else do I have to do now that I'm retired?" she said with a laugh.

"These old photographs are amazing. Is this Royal's family with his parents, Clara and John?" I asked.

"It sure is. They had five children and that's the only picture we could find of all of them together. I'd be happy to make you a copy to take back home with you," she said.

"That would be so great. Thank you!" I replied with enthusiasm.

It was neat looking through all the stuff she had, especially since I had just seen Clara's and John's grave. It reminded me that I had to ask her about Royal's headstone. I was hoping she had more information for me. Maybe he was never buried at Center Cemetery and was in some other place.

"Brady and I visited Center Cemetery where John and Clara are buried," I said.

"Oh yes, they have their family stone there. It's a nice little cemetery in the middle of nowhere, isn't it?"

"It really is. I felt very much at peace when I was there. I did have one question about something peculiar. My grandmother had told me she bought a stone for her father about ten years ago, but when I was walking around Center Cemetery I couldn't find his stone. I didn't know if maybe Royal was buried with Clara and John and *that* would be the stone my grandmother had bought?" I asked.

Freda looked like she was bursting with knowledge. I couldn't have come all this way just to see a box full of old pictures and death certificates.

"There is a reason you didn't see a stone for Royal, Anna. How much time do you have today?" she asked.

"I have as much time as you need. I came all this way to see you," I explained.

"We need to take a ride so I can explain things a bit better. Are you and Brady up for a little drive?"

I looked over at Brady and he said, "We are up for anything, Mrs. Anderson."

"I'm sure glad you said it like that," she replied with a smile that was almost bantering.

The mystery continued. What did this woman know and where in the world was she taking us? Was Royal buried someplace else and why? Maybe he was actually cremated or put in one of those aboveground tombs. The possibilities were endless.

"Okay kids, I'm just going to grab my purse and we can go," she said as she went up the stairs.

I looked around her house some more. Every room had a theme and it was perfect. Aunt Vivian would fit right in here. We walked out the front door and got into her fully loaded Mercedes.

Brady was in awe and said, "Mrs. Anderson, I have to say, you have impeccable taste in cars."

She replied with a laugh and said, "The credit must be given to my husband. He's a cardiologist and is very selective about taking care of his patients and things with four wheels."

"Wow, a cardiologist. He must be a brilliant man," I said.

"He surely is. He married *me*, didn't he?" she said with a hearty laugh.

We pulled out of the driveway and Freda asked, "What do you think of Dunkirk?"

"It's a very quaint town," I replied.

"It's a town where if you blink, you'll miss it. We only have about a thousand residents," she explained.

A thousand, yet she found a cardiologist to marry.

"Sounds like my town," Brady said.

"Where do you reside in Ohio?" she asked.

"I live in a little town called Yellow Springs," he answered.

"I've never heard of it," Freda replied as she fixed her mirrors.

"See, you must have blinked and missed it while going through Ohio," Brady joked.

"I have been to Cleveland before with my husband for a convention but we flew there," she explained.

"Well, Cleveland is definitely a bigger city and about two hundred miles from where I live."

"Big cities are overrated anyway," Freda expressed. "I like my small town. It has everything I need for survival."

"This is true," Brady replied.

I loved how he could talk to anyone. He made conversations seem so easy.

We drove for about ten minutes when Freda said we were just about there. When we turned up a driveway I noticed a sign that said "White Oaks." I had no idea what this place was. It looked like some sort of condo complex. She pulled up toward the front of the building and parked in the first available handicap spot.

"Okay, here comes the revealing part and why I sent that letter. You kids ready?" she asked.

Revealing? What was she going to reveal? I had to admit, I was a bit nervous. "I'm ready," I said with a lump in my throat.

Brady grabbed hold of my hand and we walked into this establishment. I wished I had brought the Pepto-Bismol as my stomach started to churn. Freda walked over to the front desk and the guy there knew her immediately. She asked him to call some woman.

"We just have to wait for Caroline Jones and she'll explain everything," Freda said.

Caroline Jones. She was the person who was going to tell me about this mysterious letter? She obviously worked at this place but who was she? It was a bit aggravating that she couldn't just blurt it out. What was up with all this secrecy and involvement with others? I looked around the building and saw all kinds of individuals. Some of these people seemed like they were mentally ill or something. It made me feel uncomfortable.

"It's going to be just fine, Anna," Brady said as he wrapped his arms around me.

He must have sensed my discomfort with this whole thing. I heard a voice call out to Freda and I assumed it was Caroline. They shook hands and walked toward us. Caroline was a good looking blonde woman who seemed very classy. Her welcoming smile almost gave me a sense of encouragement.

"Caroline, this is Anna Corolla and her friend Brady," Freda explained. "Anna received my letter that was addressed to her grandmother, Jean, in Connecticut. She has driven out here to learn about the news."

Caroline looked surprised and said, "Okay, well, let's go to a conference room where we can talk privately."

We followed Caroline toward the back of the building where the elevators were. We went up to the fourth floor and she led us into a conference room.

"I will be right back so make yourselves comfortable. I need to go grab my paperwork. Can I offer anyone a cup of coffee or some water maybe?"

"We will take some water, thank you," Brady spoke up. Brady then pulled out a chair for me to sit. He took the seat next to me and held my hand.

My heart began to race. This whole trip consisted of my heart racing. I wondered if I would return back home with high blood pressure or something. Brady took my hand and held it tight. I was so relieved he was there with me. I don't think I could do it on my own. It seemed like it took Caroline forever to return to the room. When she did, she had a file folder that looked pretty full. Caroline sat down at the table and began to speak.

"Freda, how do you want to handle this? Would you like to explain it to Anna or would you like me to do the honors?"

The honors? What could they possibly be talking about?

Freda spoke first and said, "I can start explaining and then maybe you can take over when we get to the technical stuff."

Caroline said, "Before we start, Anna, I need to ask you if I can see some sort of photo ID?"

A photo ID? I opened up my purse and pulled out my driver's license. "This is all I have," I said as I handed it over to Caroline. She took it from me, wrote down some information, and then handed it back to me.

"This is fine. The driver's license is perfect," she said.

As I looked over at Brady, I could tell he was getting a bit curious as well.

Freda began speaking and said, "Anna, you asked me where Royal's stone was and I plan to explain all of that to you. When I started looking into the genealogy information I never thought in a million years I would discover what I did. Like you saw in my box, I found all sorts of things on our family. There was one puzzle piece missing, as you also noticed, in regard to Royal's gravesite. I, too, visited Center Cemetery and noticed the same thing you did. I thought, 'Where is this man's grave?' I was able to locate all the other passed family member's gravesites. Not all of them are buried in Center Cemetery, but the more I researched Royal's, the more it intrigued me to find it. One afternoon I was at City Hall in Portland, trying to figure out where Royal could be buried. The girls in there were of no help to me. Then an older gentleman approached me and said he overheard me looking for Roy Schroll's gravesite. He told me I would never find it. I couldn't understand what he meant by that. I asked him if he was cremated or if he was buried by someone secretly. He just shook his head and asked me to take a ride with him. The man led me to this place, White Oaks. Like you, I had no idea why this man brought me here. He didn't speak a word to me and just told me to follow him. So I did," Freda explained.

Brady and I listened intently and at that moment I wished my father was there with me. All of a sudden, Freda had gotten choked up and a tear fell down her face. She was having a hard time getting out whatever was to come next. I almost fell out of my chair at what she said next.

"The gentleman led me into a room where an elderly man was sitting in a chair looking out the window. I asked him why I was here and he told me because I would never find Roy in the cemetery. He was sitting right over there in that chair."

There was no oxygen in that room. I couldn't find any air to breathe. *Did Freda just tell me that my great-grandfather was alive?* I spoke the only words I could get out, "It's a mistake. My grandmother lost her father when she was nine years old. He died in some factory accident. That's why she moved to Connecticut. I'm sorry but I think you have the wrong guy."

"I thought so too," said Freda. "So we followed up with DNA

testing. They did quite a few tests to confirm."

If ever I was in complete shock, now was that time. "I don't understand. How could something like this have happened?" I asked frantically.

Freda explained that the old man was a good friend of my great-grandfather and they both worked together at the factory.

"He was there the day of the accident. Royal was in bad shape and had gone into a coma. He wasn't getting any better so instead of telling the kids that their father was a vegetable, it was easier for them to move on. Royal's parents were not happy about this decision so they threatened to take the kids away from their mother. She didn't want that to happen so she moved to Connecticut where her sister resided."

"I just can't believe this. How am I supposed to make this all better?" I began to cry.

My poor grandmother had lived her entire life without ever knowing her father was still alive. Why did she have to die and not witness this? Why am I here and not her? I was helpless. I had the same feeling the night she passed away. Here I was learning that my great-grandfather is alive and in this building, while the rest of my family is eight hundred miles away. The guilt began to set in. I knew I had to pull myself together.

"What's my great-grandfather like now?" I asked.

Caroline took over and explained all the medical details to me.

"He was in a coma for years. In fact, he didn't fully come out of it until he was seventy-two years old. What I mean is, he opened his eyes five years after he went into the coma but didn't speak or walk. Your great-grandfather had to learn everything all over again. Doctors worked with him on things such as eating with a fork, getting dressed, taking a shower, and even how to walk again. It took many years for him to regain most of his activities of daily living."

"Does he remember anything?" I was almost scared to ask.

"He could tell me the street he lived on and where he worked. What he doesn't remember is the accident and who his family is. There was no recollection of him knowing his wife or even his parents. Normally with these situations, it is helpful to have photographs to show the patients so that it triggers their memory. With Royal, we had nothing to work with other than what an elderly man had told us."

"What about the elderly man? Couldn't he have helped?" I asked.

Caroline responded and said, "The man's name is John Macklebee and he was a friend and worked with Royal. John didn't know much about your family though, which made it difficult. We learned much more about Royal when Freda showed up with her genealogy research. That's when she said she was going to try and locate his daughter, Jeanie."

Hearing her tell me she tried to contact my grandmother made it much worse. That letter just sat in the drawer and it would have changed her life. It was the most bittersweet news I could have ever received. I just keep asking myself why. My grandmother could have been with the one person in the whole world that she missed so much, if only she had opened that damn letter. *Why me? Why was I the one that had to learn of this news?*

The night my grandmother passed away, I had hoped that it was her father coming for her. I wanted him to be the one who would welcome her into Heaven so she wouldn't be scared. I imagined her running into his arms and feeling his warm embrace. Now that I know it wasn't her father, who did welcome her into Heaven? Was it her mother or her sister? Maybe it was Jesus and God. I really needed some sort of tranquilizer. I took a few deep breaths and wiped my eyes and nose with a tissue and put my head up. All three of them were staring at me with compassion in their eyes.

I cleared my throat, "I'm sorry I'm so upset and emotional. It's just that my grandmother loved her father so much and it pained her to lose him. Now I learn that he has been alive this entire time and she missed out. It's really, really, bad timing."

Freda spoke up and said, "Life is funny, isn't it? Sometimes it can be a cruel joke or just simply a mystery. I'm sorry that your grandmother couldn't have seen her father again. I'm sure she was busy with her family. Taking care of Royal at the time would have been a lot of work for her. I'm not saying she wouldn't have done it because I can guarantee she would have. I am going to use a saying that is always overused but is very true and that is, 'everything happens for a reason'. You told me your family is in turmoil and you needed this escape.

Anna, look what you are going home with. I am not sure how your family will take this news, but they get a piece of your grandmother back and now they get a chance to know their grandfather, if they choose to."

Freda was right. With my voice trembling and tears still rolling down my cheeks, I asked her, "How do I tell them?"

Caroline piped up and said, "With news this big, it's best if they come here and we talk face to face like you did."

She was right but how in the world would I get them all here? After all, I totally lied about my entire trip.

"Can I see him?" I asked.

Caroline put her hand over mine and said, "Absolutely, Anna."

Freda then said, "I can take her to go meet him, Caroline. Maybe it would be easier to explain who she is if I bring her in."

"That's a great idea," Caroline replied.

"Do you want me to stay with you or is this something you want to do on your own?" Brady asked.

"I think I will be okay. Maybe you should go call home to check on your mom," I suggested.

"You read my mind," he said as he kissed my forehead and walked out of the room.

"Okay darling, are you ready to go meet your great-grandpa?" Freda asked.

I knew I had to be strong. I didn't want Royal to sense my sadness. I wanted this to be a good visit and one I would never forget.

"Sure, I'm ready, Freda," I said, as I touched her arm. "Thank you."

She wrapped an arm around me and said, "You're very welcome dear."

* * *

We took the elevators up to the ninth floor. She said they have him on the ninth floor because he likes the view of the farmlands. There is also a little pond outside his window with ducks that swim in it and he likes to watch them too. I have to admit I was nervous. *What was I going to say to him?* I knew nothing about him other than stories my

156

grandmother told and he was only in his thirties at that time. The man was now ninety-six years old. According to Caroline, he was in remarkable shape and aside from the accident and coma, he was healthy and not on any meds.

We walked down the hallway and she told me his room was all the way at the end. It was more private down there. Freda visited my great-grandpa every week. She would bring him food and she'd show him her genealogy box. I was grateful for her and how she took care of him.

"Are you ready?" she asked.

"I am," I said, even though in my mind I was thinking no.

"Knock, Knock," Freda said as she opened up Royal's door.

I could hear his voice slightly as I walked in behind her. She went over to him and gave him a kiss on the cheek. I looked at him and saw him smile. He had my grandmother's smile. The way he greeted Freda showed me that he was definitely her father. He was pleasant and sweet and reached out his arms to offer her a hug. My grandmother hugged everyone and her hugs were the best. Royal was medium-sized and he didn't look a year over eighty. Freda called me over and started the introduction.

"Uncle Roy, there is someone really special I'd like you to meet," Freda said in a louder voice so he could hear. She motioned me over to her.

"This is your great-granddaughter, Anna." I looked into my great-grandpa's eyes and they were hazel, just like my grandmother's.

When I saw how joyous he was to learn that I was his granddaughter, it melted my heart. He got up from his chair and wrapped his arms around me. I was amazed at how well he was able to get out of the chair at his age. When I hugged him, I was hugging my grandmother. I knew I had to say something but I was choked up and couldn't talk. This moment was like a dream come true and I was at a loss for words.

"I don't know what to say. It's a miracle that I found you. I'm overjoyed to have this moment," I said as I put my hand over his.

"I can't believe it," he said. "I have a granddaughter. You folks just made my day. Thank you, Freda, for bringing her to visit me," he said.

"I'm going to leave you two alone for a few minutes so you can get acquainted," said Freda and she left the room.

There I was, sitting in a room with my great-grandfather, who I thought had died back in 1940. All those years I would look up at the antique picture of him that my grandmother had on her wall. It's amazing to think that he was here the entire time getting better each day that passed. I couldn't help but stare at him and make the comparisons between him and my grandmother.

"So, tell me about yourself, Anna," he said.

"That would take all day, but I'll try my best," I joked. "I'm twenty-three, just graduated from college, and I live in Connecticut."

"Connecticut? Why does your family live in Connecticut?" he asked with surprise.

I didn't know how to answer him. I couldn't tell him the truth. "Sometimes I ask myself that very same question," I replied.

"Would you tell me about the family," he asked.

"Your daughter, Jeanie, is my grandmother. She has a son named Frank and Frank is my father. Jeanie also has two daughters, Viviane and Sharon. Sharon doesn't have children but Viviane has two boys. I'm an only child." I was probably confusing the man so I took out my phone to show him pictures. "I have some pictures if you'd like to see," I said.

He smiled back at me and said, "I would love to see pictures of my family."

Luckily, my phone has a big screen so he could see them well enough. I showed him some pictures from my graduation and our last family Easter. He really was enjoying them until he asked where his Jeanie was. I felt that lump in my throat again but I had to be strong.

"My grandmother passed away a few months ago," I blurted out.

He looked as if he had just lost his best friend. I hated that moment more than anything.

"I'm so sorry. I wish it was her sitting here meeting you. She spoke of you all the time and how much she missed you," I explained as I felt a teardrop sneak out of my right eye.

"It's okay, Anna. Were you close with her?" he asked.

"Very. She was like a mother to me and you would have been very proud of her," I explained as more tears got loose.

He handed me a tissue from his end table. "It's okay to cry," he said. "I don't remember much about that time of my life. The medicine they are giving me allows me to have more recent memory but to go back to the early days is hard."

He looked as if something was bothering him.

"There is one memory I have and I dream it sometimes. I'm not sure if it is real or just in my head. I remember the cutest little girl with short brown hair jumping off a tire swing and running into my arms," he said with a smile and a tear.

That was it. I officially lost it. It felt like a hose was filling my eyes and the tears then poured out.

"That was her," I said. It was all I could get out at the moment. My great-grandpa put his arm around me and we sat there for a minute trying to collect our emotions.

"My grandmother would tell me the tire swing story all the time. She said she would swing on it and wait for you to come home from work. She loved telling that story," I said.

"Well, I am glad it's not just a dream then because it really is the only thing I can remember," he said.

"If my grandmother knew you were still alive, she would have rushed here. Please know this," I explained.

"Thank you, Anna. I hope she lived a good life."

"She did. Her husband is still alive and our family is really close. She was the glue that held us together though," I said.

"I hope to meet them all someday," he said.

"I definitely think you will. This is a true family phenomenon. We lost someone who meant so much to us and with you, it's like we are getting a piece back," I explained.

"Well, I appreciate that. The hardest part about life is death. But we all have to face it one day. I will look forward to that day so I can see my little girl again," he said.

I wanted to cry so hard. I felt the way he did. When she passed away, all I could think of was that one day when my turn comes, I hope I see her face with her arms wide open. Just then we were interrupted by the staff.

"Mr. Schroll, it's your lunchtime. I'm here to walk you down to the cafeteria," the staff lady said.

"Okay Sue, but what about Anna?" he asked.

"Anna is going back with Freda for a little while but don't worry, you will see her again," Sue said.

"That's good. Hey Sue, I got me a beautiful granddaughter." He smiled as he hugged me farewell.

I loved him already. I went back down to the conference room where Freda and Caroline were waiting. Caroline asked me about the family.

"I assume you are going to share this information with the rest of your family?"

"I will call them and see if I can get them to fly here. They have to," I said.

Brady walked back into the conference room. He came over to me and clenched me in his arms. "Do you want to go to the hotel and rest a bit? You've had a rather interesting morning."

Brady was right. I needed some time to adapt. I had to call my family but I wanted to do it in private, not here.

"It was lovely to meet you, Anna. Please let me know if you need anything," Caroline said as she shook my hand.

"Thank you very much, you've been more than helpful," I replied.

Freda drove us back to her house and we said our goodbyes. I told her I would let her know how I make out with my family. "I am hopeful that my dad and his sisters will fly here. I can't possibly explain all of this over the phone. If I get them here, I will be sure to let you know," I explained.

She hugged me and said, "God only gives us what we can handle dear."

I smiled at her and said, "My grandmother always said that."

* * *

Back at the hotel we ordered room service but I wasn't all that hungry. I had to figure out a way to get my family to fly out to Indiana. "What if they don't come?" I asked Brady.

"Then they miss out on a mind-boggling discovery," he said. "Anna, you can only lead the horses to water. We can't always make them drink. I know you will give it your best effort."

"What if they get mad at me?" I asked.

"They won't or shouldn't. Do you think if any one of them found that letter they would come all the way out here like you did?"

Brady made a great point. If anything, they probably would have called and heard it over the phone. Brady continued with his inspirational thoughts.

"Furthermore, what if you didn't find that letter? It could have taken years to find, if at all. Your family would never know your great-grandpa is alive."

"You are right. I shouldn't be afraid to call them. In fact, they should be thankful," I said.

"They should be," Brady said as he took a bite of his room service pasta.

Brady decided to go to the hotel gym and workout so I could have some time to call my family. For a moment, I felt like I was frozen in time. I had to sink all this information in. *This whole thing has to be a dream. It would be the only logical explanation for all of this.*

All of a sudden my cell was ringing. Nope, I definitely wasn't dreaming. I looked at the screen and it was from Dad. A part of me was afraid to answer but I had to face this eventually.

"Hello," I answered.

"Anna, it's Dad. I've been thinking about you all day. Are you almost done with your Chicago sightseeing?"

"Not exactly," I replied.

"What's wrong? You don't sound like yourself," he said with deep concern.

I took a deep breath and just blurted it out. "Dad, I lied to you. I'm not in Chicago. I'm in Indiana, and Brady is with me."

He interrupted me before I could say any more. "Anna, what in the world were you thinking? You're a smart woman, but this has got to be the dumbest thing you could do. You barely know this Brady character."

I ignored his comment about Brady and continued on. I knew if I didn't I would never get it out.

"The night we went to Poppy's and I printed my thesis paper, I found a letter. It was addressed to Grandma from someone in Indiana and it was unopened. I know I shouldn't have taken it but I got so mad at you all for arguing and I threw it in my bag." The phone was quiet for a few seconds. "Dad? Are you still there?"

"Yes, Anna, I'm here. I'm trying to understand what you just said to me," he replied calmly.

"After I opened the letter, I realized it was from a cousin in Indiana who was trying to reach Grandma. The letter mentioned she had important news for her. I guess she tried to call her but couldn't locate a number as their phone is unlisted. After I opened it and read it, I had to take this trip." I explained.

"I'm not sure I am following you, Anna. What did the note say to make you drive halfway across the country and lie to me?"

"It didn't tell me anything other than that there was news."

"Well, what was the news?" he asked.

"That's the hard part, Dad. I can't tell you because you need to be here, as does Auntie Sharon and Aunt Vivian. In fact, I need you guys to get here as soon as you can," I said.

"Anna, are you in some kind of trouble, or hurt?" he asked with fear in his voice.

"Dad," my voice cracked as the tears started to roll. "The most unexplainable thing has happened. I need all of you guys to trust me and just get here. You know me, Dad. I wouldn't tell you guys to come all the way to Indiana unless it was for a good reason. In fact, I'll even pay for your plane tickets."

"Anna, it is not about the money. You have to understand what it sounds like to me on the other end. My daughter took off halfway across the U.S. Her car breaks down and she runs off with some strange guy to Indiana to find a cousin we've never met because of a letter that contains some news. I don't know, Anna. I will be there because I'm your father and I need you home safe. And I'll do what I can as far as Auntie Sharon and Aunt Vivian are concerned."

"Dad, the news has to do with everyone. They have to come. Please, do whatever is necessary," I pleaded.

"I'll try, Anna. What town are we coming to?" he asked.

"Portland," I replied.

"I'll call you when we land," he said as he hung up.

CHAPTER SIXTEEN

"Good morning, Sunshine," Brady said as he kissed my forehead.

I was lying in bed and had just woken up. "What time is it?" I asked him.

"It's nine-thirty," he answered.

"Nine thirty?" I said with surprise. "I don't even remember falling asleep."

"When I came back from the gym you were passed out with your phone lying next to you in bed. I assumed the conversation with your dad wiped you out. I put your phone back on the charge and tucked you in," he explained.

I had almost forgotten about all the craziness when I saw his face. He took me away to a whole new place.

"I talked to your dad this morning. It was by accident, really. Your phone was going off and you were sleeping so peacefully. I tried to stop it from ringing and then realized your dad was on the line," he said.

"Oh my gosh. What did he say?" I asked.

He brushed my hair behind my shoulders and said, "It was fine. And you will be happy to know that your Auntie Sharon, your Aunt Vivian, and your father are all headed here now on an airplane. They should be landing around one-thirty."

I smiled at him and gave him a huge hug. I was so relieved that he was with me. "You keep rescuing me and I hope I'm not tiring you out," I said.

He kissed my lips so flawlessly and said, "You've rescued *me*, Anna."

* * *

That morning, as we sat in the Coffee Cup Café having our breakfast, I felt peaceful and calm. I knew my family was on their way and even though it would be emotional for them, somehow I knew I did the right thing. Aunt Sharon would be beyond emotional because like me, she was the closest to Grandma. And although I knew it would be hard for her at first, in the end she was getting a piece of her mother back.

"Are you nervous to see your family?" Brady asked as he took a sip of his espresso.

"I'm more nervous that they will be upset at me for lying but it is what it is. We get to know someone who we thought died over sixty years ago. How often do people get to say they witnessed something like this?" I said.

"This story would make for a good blockbuster hit."

He was right. This was something that would make a good movie. It was surreal.

"I've witnessed a miracle recently too," Brady said. "It was the afternoon I found you sitting in the pouring rain next to your car."

"Is it possible to fall in love so quickly?" I asked.

"Love is a strong word, Anna, but if there was a word that was stronger, it would define us," he answered.

I felt a little confused. Was he saying that what we had was stronger than love? He definitely needed to go to school in Boston. His use of words was poetic.

My family was meeting us at the hotel. I called a limo service to bring us over to White Oaks. I wanted all of us to drive over together. They would be arriving around 2:30 p.m. The time was moving so slowly. Brady and I tried to stall time by browsing through a few stores. He surprised me with a Portland, Indiana T-shirt. "You should have a souvenir from your trip," he said.

"What about you? I think you deserve one too," I replied.

"Oh, I bought one too. I figured we could match," he pulled out his identical shirt and we joked.

Finally, it was time. I saw a Lincoln Town Car pull up to the hotel and I watched my family exit the vehicle. I have to admit, I was relieved to see them. My dad came through the entrance first and ran over to hug me.

"Anna, oh I am so glad you're okay," he said as he squeezed me to a point where I couldn't breathe.

I then introduced him to Brady. "Dad, this is the man that deserves all your attention because he has taken very good care of me."

"It's nice to meet you, Mr. Corolla. You have raised an exceptional daughter. You should be very proud," Brady said as he shook my father's hand. He looked so nervous but he did great.

"Brady, it's a pleasure to meet you and I cannot thank you enough for keeping her safe because she is my world," my dad replied.

"Auntie Sharon, Aunt Vivian, thank you guys so much for coming. In a little while you will be able to make some sense out of this urgent trip," I said as I hugged them both. I then introduced them to Brady as well.

My Auntie Sharon whispered into my ear, "Anna, he's arresting."

She always liked to use unique words. Instead of simply saying he's attractive, she uses a word like "arresting." We laughed as I walked them all to the elevators. I had them leave their bags in our room and take a potty break before we got into the limo.

"You hired us a limo?" Aunt Vivian asked.

"I wanted all of us to go together so this was a good option," I replied.

"You are my niece," she replied with pride.

"So this is Portland, eh?" my dad said as he was looking out the window.

"Yes, isn't it great, Dad?"

"From what I see so far, it's not overly country-looking here."

"Portland is a cute little town with many modern amenities but the second you leave here, it's all cornfields and tobacco," I said laughing.

"We saw a lot of those on the way here from the airport."

"My mother always talked about Indiana. I can't believe we're here. I wish I knew where she lived," my Aunt Sharon said.

"I do," I replied. "I went to the house and even sat in what I think was her old tire swing"

"Really?" Aunt Vivian asked with much surprise.

"Yes, it was amazing and the lady who lives there now was so hospitable," I said.

"I'd like to see it, Anna," Aunt Sharon said.

"I definitely can take you there. I first need to show you why you're here though," I said.

The limo ride seemed to take awhile. I wondered if they were upset with me about the letter. I had to say something about it. "I'm really sorry I took the letter and didn't tell anyone," I said.

My Aunt Vivian spoke up and said, "It's quite alright, Anna. Who could blame you? That night wasn't our finest moment. I need to apologize for a lot of my actions lately. I don't like to feel the sadness so I try hard not to give into my emotions."

I couldn't believe Aunt Vivian just said that. They were the most heartfelt words I had ever heard her speak. Not that she was a bad person. She just wasn't overly affectionate.

There are people like that in this world. It doesn't make them bad people. I felt bad for her in a way. I know I had a lot of anger toward her about the will but she wasn't one to cry in front of us or share her feelings. Maybe she was taking it the worst because of that. Sometimes just a hug makes me feel ten times better and she can't get that same satisfaction.

My father responded to my Aunt Viv's comment and said, "We all loved her and it's been a rough time for all of us. The important thing is we are still family and have to find a way to make it work."

As we pulled into the parking lot of White Oaks, my family looked puzzled. I smiled at my dad as he put his arm around me.

"Okay, here we are," said the limo driver as he opened the door for us.

"Thank you so much, sir," I replied.

"No problem, young lady. I will be back around 5:00 p.m. to pick you up" he said.

"I'm going to stay out here in the courtyard," Brady whispered to me. "It's important for you to do this with your family." I kissed his cheek and took my father by the hand.

Caroline was at the front desk, ready to take us up. "Hello Anna," she said. I introduced her to the family.

"Your cousin Freda is already upstairs in the conference room, so follow me," Caroline said.

When we walked into the room, Freda stood up with a big smile.

"Hi Freda," I said and gave her a hug. "This is my Dad, Frank, and his two sisters, Sharon and Vivian."

She walked over to them and gave them all cheerful handshakes. "It is so nice to meet my cousins," she said.

"Why don't we all sit down and get started," Caroline suggested.

I took a seat between my dad and Aunt Sharon.

"Thank you all for flying out here so quickly. I know you must be wondering what this is all about. First, you should be proud of Anna. If it weren't for her finding that letter, none of this would be possible," Caroline said.

My dad squeezed my hand with pride.

"I am going to turn it over to Freda for a minute so she can explain the first part," Caroline said.

"My mother, Goldie, was your grandfather's sister, which would make her your great-aunt. I lost my mother three years ago, which began my interest in genealogy. I found some interesting facts about our family so I continued to dig deeper. I gathered old pictures and birth certificates and sadly, the obituaries too. They are all right here in this box that you all can look through later. As I was doing my research, I would often visit cemeteries and look up old relatives. I went to Center Cemetery just like Anna did to look for my grandparents, John and Clara. They were Goldie and Royal's parents. I also wanted to see my Uncle Royal's stone. I grew up in Michigan so I didn't know much about Royal's family. When I arrived at the cemetery, I couldn't find his stone. I went down to City Hall and an elderly man overheard my conversation asking about Royal's grave. He told me that he knew where he was. That man brought me here to White Oaks."

My family looked confused but continued to pay close attention as Caroline stood up to take over.

"When Freda came here with the man, he brought her to our courtyard where many of our patients like to sit and enjoy the outdoors. He then told her that his friend Earl was over there under the tree. Freda was confused as she didn't notice anyone buried under that tree. She only noticed a gentleman sitting in a chair."

My Aunt Sharon interrupted abruptly and said, "Wait, wait a minute. Are you trying to tell us that our grandfather is alive? That is impossible because he died when my mother was nine years old."

Aunt Sharon was getting tense and I could tell the tears would be coming soon. Both my dad and Aunt Vivian looked clueless.

Caroline then said, "He never died in that work accident. He had gone into a deep coma. Back then, when someone had gone into a coma like he had, they would either pass away or basically be a vegetable. Your grandmother decided it was best for the family to assume he was gone to Heaven because medically, he was never going to be the same.

"This can't be. This simply cannot be true. My mother would have known if her own father was alive," Aunt Sharon said with tears bursting out of her eyes.

Aunt Vivian spoke up and said, "How do we know for sure this is our grandfather?"

"Medical is so enhanced nowadays and we were able to match his DNA. I know this is hard and overwhelming for all of you but you needed to know."

My dad finally said something. "Is he here now? Is he alive?"

Caroline replied with a smile and said, "He is and he's doing quite well for a man in his nineties. Royal doesn't recall much from his childhood or his married life, but he is fully capable now of conversation and has the ability to remember short-term events."

"So he would have no idea who we are?" Aunt Sharon asked with a shake in her voice.

I handed her a tissue and said, "Auntie Sharon, he will understand who you are when you tell him. I met him yesterday and he is amazing, just like Grandma was. And he does remember one thing about his married life. He remembers a little girl on that tire swing," I barely got the words out before crying.

My dad was comforting me by rubbing my back. Aunt Vivian sat there and stared at the wall. I got out of my chair and went over to hug her. She also started tearing up, then went into a full blown crying session. I had never seen anything like it.

Caroline brought us all tissues and water. She knew we would need some time to process the information. Freda tried to comfort us as well. She was a nice lady. Not only did we get a grandfather, but we gained a cousin too.

My aunts had calmed down and Caroline asked if they wanted to meet him. It was a little before dinner so he would be outside in the courtyard. We walked down there and I found Brady. He joined us. We stopped at the door that led us outside.

"Is that him?" Aunt Sharon asked when she saw a man waving over at Caroline.

"That's your grandfather," she replied with a smile.

Caroline introduced everyone to Royal. He was smiling ear to ear and I could tell he was overwhelmed with happiness.

"You have my mother's eyes," Aunt Sharon told him.

He simply replied with a laugh, "I think she had mine."

During our visit we talked about Grandma a lot. Royal loved listening to everyone share things about her. My aunts also had pictures of her on their phone and he loved seeing her. There were lots and lots of hugs and I was getting the feeling that Aunt Vivian was getting used to them too. The chain that was broken was in the process of being fixed and it was all thanks to that letter and Freda's interest in genealogy. I know my grandmother was looking down on us and smiling. I had a feeling it was all of her angelic signs that led us to this moment.

I wasn't sure how we would ever go back to Connecticut and leave Royal here. My Aunt Vivian asked him if he would ever consider moving.

He said, "Home is where my family is."

He was right. My Aunt Vivian assured him that she would be in touch. If he was interested in moving to Connecticut to be with us, we would do whatever it took. Freda agreed to help us because she knew how much it meant for us to have him back in our lives. I had a feeling that she was now going to be a big part of our lives too.

"We received an amazing gift here today and it is something I will never forget. Thank you, Ma," Aunt Vivian said as she looked up to the sky.

I even saw Aunt Sharon and Aunt Vivian share a hug. Brady and I went for a short walk while my dad and aunts enjoyed their visit.

"So what now?" Brady asked.

"I don't know. It seems like everything falls into place when we don't make plans," I said as we walked hand in hand around the pond. We sat on the bench and continued to talk.

"I know why my grandfather likes the ducks in the pond. Their life seems so simple," I said.

"Life is simple, if you let it be," Brady said. "But those ducks in the pond follow each other around. They don't have decisions to make like we do."

"True, very true," I said.

"I can't just let you go back to Connecticut and see what happens," he said. "I want to see what this is between us." He sat for a moment and then said, "What if I spend the summer in Connecticut? I can rent an apartment and find a job and then maybe I will look into Boston for the fall?"

"What about your family, Brady? They are important to you," I said.

"They are but they can't be my future. I don't want to be some forty-year-old man living at home with his parents because he let the most amazing girl get away. I want to pursue her. What if I stay in Ohio and then realize after it's too late that *you* were my letter, my destiny? We met by chance and what this is just feels right to me," he said with such passion and conviction.

I looked at this man and knew that if I went back home and left him in Ohio I, too, would regret it. "I'm scared and I don't want you to lose your family because of me," I said as I stroked his cheek.

He grabbed my hand and said, "If I lost my family over you, then they were never a good family to begin with. Like your family has shown me today, it's about supporting each other. They love me and want me to be happy. My happiness is with you," he explained.

My life was taking all kinds of crazy turns. This road trip brought me an amazing boyfriend, a new cousin, and a great-grandfather. I was sure that I would soon be hit by a bus. All these great things don't just happen. There has to be some sort of bad karma coming my way. Or was it that I was finally learning to enjoy my life? Maybe it was my grandma showering me with happiness because I had forgotten what that was for awhile.

I stood up from that bench, smiled down at Brady, and said, "Yes, I want you to come with me and I want to kiss you every day."

He jumped off that bench so fast, wrapped me in his arms, and twirled me around. It was another moment that only happens in the movies, and I was taking full advantage of it. Just as I was starring in a new romance film in my mind, I heard Aunt Sharon's voice calling me over.

"Brady, can I borrow my Godchild for a moment?" she asked.

"Sure," he said with a little blush of embarrassment.

"You really like him, huh, Anna?" Aunt Sharon asked.

"I know it sounds crazy, but I do. In fact, he is going to come to Connecticut for the summer and may take some classes at B.U. in the fall," I said.

She smiled and said, "I'm glad he makes you happy. Hold on to that feeling as long as you can, my dear."

"I will, thanks," I said as I gave her a hug.

"Anna, I wanted to pull you aside so you know how very proud I am of you and how proud your grandmother would have been. I'm still in shock over the news you discovered but I'm so thankful," she said with a few tears strolling down her cheek.

"I'm just sorry I didn't find it sooner so that Grandma could have been here to be with her dad," I said with a tear.

She put her arm around me tightly and said, "Grandma *is* here, Anna. She led you right back to her roots in Indiana."

THE END

BLACK ROSE writing™

CPSIA information can be obtained at www.ICGtesting.com
Printed in the USA
BVOW06s1421120815

413077BV00021B/149/P

9 781612 963679